Fundamental Leadership and Engineering Competencies

P.K. Raju
Thomas Walter Professor, Department of Mechanical
Engineering, Auburn University

Chetan S. Sankar
Department of Management, Auburn University

Qiang Le
Assistant Professor, Hampton University

ISBN: 978-1-937435-45-5

May He protect us both (the teacher and the student) together by revealing knowledge. May He protect us both by assuring that knowledge will be used fruitfully. May we be vigorous in learning together. Let what we study be invigorating to both of us. May we not criticize each other needlessly. Om Peace, Peace, Peace.

Katha Upanishad

This book is dedicated to...

- Our teachers who have inspired us throughout life
- National Science Foundation for being a leader in supporting innovative educational practices
- Our students who have participated with us in this project and worked tirelessly
- Our friends in industry who supported us by providing vital information
- Our families who gave the time and support to make this book a reality.

Published by
Tavenner Publishing Company
406 Sutton Place
Anderson, SC 29625
864-617-4449
fax- 864-751-5855
tavpubco@charter.net

Fundamental Leadership and Engineering Competencies

Table of Contents

1. INTRODUCTION

Learning Goals

After you have read and studied this chapter, you should be able to:

- Learn how engineers interact with scientists, mathematicians, and business people to develop products that transform our lives
- Obtain an overview of some of the major engineering achievements of the 20th century
- Understand the contributions of different engineering disciplines
- Learn about major professional societies
- Learn what is expected of engineering students in the 21st century
- Learn how multimedia case studies will help you meet the new skill expectations

1.1 Science, Technology, and Engineering

The label that is applied to an object or concept can be very revealing. For example, the word "science" comes from the Latin word *scientia*, which means knowledge, and a scientist identifies what is known about things and puts that knowledge into some kind of order. The word "technology" combines the Greek word τεχνη (techne, or combined art and skill) with the ending ~ology (the lore or the science of something), so in its role as the science of making things, technology stands for the actual act of making things.

"Engineering" comes from the Latin word *ingenium*, meaning mental power, or inventiveness. Engineers are technologists who are well schooled in science and can make effective use of it through creative design processes to create engines that transform our lives and the world we live in[1]. Scientific understanding makes it possible for engineers to make robust products, mathematics makes it possible to simulate the use of the products before mass-scale production, and manufacturing processes make it possible to produce large volumes of the product. Thus, engineers must be familiar with many different scientific disciplines and be able to use that knowledge to solve practical problems. They must then work with business people to market and sell these products, thereby making the products available to the general public. Profits are made, providing an incentive for other companies to come up with improved products, which in turn leads to competition and yet more innovations.

1.2 Engineering Achievements Transform Lives

Although engineers have been transforming lives throughout recorded history, these transformations have been particularly significant during the 20th century. Their contributions have revolutionized many different areas due to innovations such as electrification, automobiles, health technologies, nuclear technologies, air travel, water supply and distribution, electronics, radio and television, agricultural mechanization, computers, telephony, air conditioning and refrigeration, highways, spacecraft, the Internet, imaging, household appliances, petroleum and

1

petrochemical technologies, lasers and fiber optics, and high performance materials. In this chapter, we focus on a few of these technologies: electrification, automobiles, health technologies, and nuclear technologies. You can refer to the publications listed at the end of the chapter to read more about the contributions of engineers to other disciplines[2]. In addition to discussing these four areas in general terms, we have included excerpts from the real-world showing in detail the impact of a few of the contributions. These examples show that the technologies by themselves are neutral; people can use them to benefit or to harm humanity. The examples from the real-world connections show that in addition to the technical challenges they face, engineers also need to be concerned about ethical issues when designing and creating new machinery and must be able to communicate their concerns to their management and to the public when appropriate.

1.2.1   Electrification

The first commercial power plant was inaugurated in 1882 by Thomas Edison, leading to massive changes in U.S. society. This opened the door for many more world-changing innovations, such as plans for electrifying the rural regions of the globe, the introduction of steam turbines, nuclear power, emission control, and plans to efficiently transmit and distribute power, all of which took place during the 20th century. The last hundred years have shown that the supply of reliable, affordable electricity is an essential prerequisite to our economic and social progress. Engineers work together to design and build power plants that provide electricity to homes and businesses. For example, electrical engineers design the generators that produce power and devise networks to transmit power, mechanical engineers design the boilers that burn coal and the steam turbines that drive the generators, chemical engineers design the nuclear reactors that drive generators, and civil engineers design the foundations and buildings that house the machinery used in a power plant. The challenges for the future stem from the fact that about two billion people worldwide still live without access to electric power. The need for an inexpensive means of generating electric power and transmitting it with minimal loss is a critical one. If electrification's next century is to be as successful as its last, we need young men and women to pursue careers in engineering and science.

1.2.2   Automobiles

During the 19th century, suburbs tended to grow in a radial pattern dictated by trolley lines; the invention of the car has allowed them to develop anywhere within commuting distance of the workplace, which is frequently in another suburb. Malls, factories, schools, fast-food restaurants, gas stations, and motels have spread out across our land with an ever-expanding road network. Today's version of daily life would be unthinkable without the personal mobility afforded by automobiles. Of the 10,000 or so cars that were on the road at the start of the 20th century, three-quarters were electric or had external combustion steam engines. However, the versatile and efficient gas-burning internal combustion engine rapidly came to dominate the road. Engineers outside of the U.S. were often in the vanguard of invention, while Americans continued to excel in the details of manufacturing. The major innovations in automobile manufacturing were: assembly line manufacturing, self starters, and disk brakes in the 1910s, safety-glass windshields in the 1920s, front-wheel drive, independent front suspension, and automatic transmission in the 1930s, tubeless and radial tires in the 1940s, electronic fuel injection in the 1960s, and electronic ignition systems in the 1970s. Concerns about safety have led to the use of seatbelts and airbags in cars, computerized braking systems, onboard microprocessors to reduce polluting emissions, and new materials to make the components lighter without compromising structural strength. Hybrid cars, powered by both gasoline and electricity, are already available. The automobile remains the most voracious consumer of cutting-edge technology and new inventions are constantly needed to enable people to enjoy nature and their preferred lifestyle in the suburbs and in the cities. However, although private ownership of automobiles is commonplace in industrialized countries, it is still a dream for many in developing countries.

Your interest and inventions are needed to make automobiles more affordable and environmentally friendly. To help you learn the skills you will need to achieve this, during your engineering education you may have an opportunity to work with new automotive designs by participating in mini-Baja teams. Mini Baja® consists of three regional competitions that simulate real-world engineering design projects and their related challenges. Engineering students are required to design and build an off-road vehicle that will survive the severe punishment of rough terrain and, in the East competition, water. There are also competitions for solar car teams, where the purpose of the project is to design and build a car that runs on solar power and students compete to win a 2,300 mile cross-country race, and Formula SAE cars. Figure 1 shows an entry in the annual Formula Society of Automotive Engineers competition to design, build and race an open-wheel racer to rigorous specifications within a tight timeline. Teams must demonstrate production costs and manufacturability, as well as market their design on its merits before proving their machine's abilities on the race track.

Figure 1 - Formula SAE Car, Auburn University, 2004

Let us now review some examples from the real-world that are related to the areas of achievements discussed in this section.

1.2.3   Health Technologies

Another area where engineering has had a major impact is in health technologies. In 1900, the average life expectancy in the US was 47 years; by 2000 it was nearing 77 years. This remarkable increase has been the result of a number of factors, including the creation of a safe water supply and a better understanding of the importance of hygiene. However, no small part of the credit should go to the century's wide array of medical advances in diagnosis, pharmaceuticals, medical devices, and other forms of treatment[3]. As the century progressed, improvements in imaging techniques wrought by the development of new systems—from x-ray machines to MRI (magnetic resonance imaging) scanners—have enabled doctors to diagnose illnesses more accurately by providing a more exact view of the body. Computers and microelectronic components have made it possible for bio-engineers to design and build prosthetic limbs that better replicate the mechanical actions of natural arms and legs. First-generation biomaterials – polymers, metals and acrylic fibers among others – have been used for almost everything from artificial heart valves and eye lenses to replacement hip, knee, elbow, and shoulder joints. Engineering has had a major impact in the operating room, developing devices such as the operating microscope, fiber-optic endoscope, and the laparoscope. These devices allow doctors to see and work inside the body without the need to surgically create large access openings, thus speeding healing time and lessening complications. Radiological catheters not only allow surgeons to see inside blood vessels, but are also used to clear blocked arteries. Lasers are now a mainstay of eye surgery and are also routinely employed to create incisions elsewhere in the body, to burn away growths, and to cauterize wounds. A robotic surgeon prototype has been developed that translates a surgeon's hand movements into more delicately tuned actions of robotic arms holding microinstruments. Health care technology and bioengineering are interdisciplinary subjects. They require ideas, people, and knowledge from all the physical sciences, all the natural sciences, all the medical sciences, all engineering disciplines, and all the photonic sciences. This diverse group of practitioners, converging under the umbrella of bioengineering, will shape the future, leading us to the greatest engineering achievements of the 21st century[4]. You will have an opportunity to participate in this exciting new area by pursuing your studies in the field of engineering.

1.2.4   Nuclear technologies

Although a cloud of doom has shadowed the future since the first atomic bomb was tested in the New Mexico desert in July 1945, the process that led to that moment also paved the way for myriad technologies that have improved the lives of millions around the world. It all began with perhaps the most famous formula of all – Albert Einstein's deceptively simple mathematical expression describing the relationship between matter and energy: $E=mc^2$, or energy equals mass multiplied by the speed of light squared. The theory supporting this equation demonstrates that under proper conditions mass can be converted to energy and, more significantly, that a very small amount of matter is equivalent to a very great deal of energy. Figure 2 shows the entrance to the Albert Einstein museum exhibit at Ulm, Germany. The two sculptures at the entrance have been designed to pay homage to Einstein on both a personal and professional level, reminding us of his famous shock of unkempt hair and also showing his formula $E=mc^2$.

Figure 2 - Sculpture showing E=mc2 in front of the Exhibit on Albert Einstein, Ulm, Germany, birthplace of Einstein, in July 2004

Physicists Enrico Fermi, Lise Meitner and Otto Frisch realized that splitting uranium atoms could lead to the release of large amounts of energy. When an atom splits it releases other neutrons, which under the right conditions could go on to split other atoms in a chain reaction. This could lead either to the steady generation of energy in the form of heat (used in nuclear power plants to produce power around the world) or a huge explosion (used in the nuclear bombs that were dropped on the Japanese cities of Hiroshima and Nagasaki in August 1945, destroying the cities and killing an estimated hundred thousand people[5]). Unlike coal and oil burning power plants, nuclear plants release neither air pollutants nor the greenhouse gases that contribute to global warming. Engineers work together with scientists to build nuclear bombs, nuclear power plants, and nuclear medicine equipment. Some 400 nuclear plants generate electricity around the world, providing 20% of the energy used in the U.S., 80% in France, and more than 50% in Japan. One ton of nuclear fuel produces the energy equivalent of 2 million to 3 million tons of fossil fuel. However, the terrorist attacks of September 2001 raised the stakes for nuclear security, and the year 2002 brought new challenges to international efforts to prevent the spread of nuclear weapons. Nuclear power has become economically competitive while simultaneously operating more safely than ever before[6]. You as an engineer may be able to contribute enormously in this area in the future.

We will now present a few real-world connections related to health and nuclear technologies. These again show that the technologies can be used to either benefit or harm people.

1.2.5   Other Engineering Innovations

The contribution of engineering to electrification, automobile, health, and nuclear technologies during the 20th century has been substantial, as shown above. In addition, significant innovations have been made in the last hundred years due to the introduction of airplanes, spacecraft, water supply and distribution systems, highways, high performance materials, electronics, computers, the Internet, telephony, radio, TV, imaging, petroleum and petrochemical technologies, textiles, and agricultural mechanization. Different disciplines of engineering have emerged as part of this progress and, as described in the next section, engineers may now choose to work in any of a wide range of specialized areas.

1.3 Engineering Disciplines

Engineering is composed of many fields of specialization. Looking at the curriculum in an engineering school during the 1950s, you might see only a few fields of engineering such as electrical, civil, and mechanical. Nowadays, however, many new fields of engineering have been added to this basic lineup as each new innovation demands new types of engineering graduates to join industry. Change is a constant in the engineering industry and this is reflected in the engineering curriculum. As you look around your home and work, almost everything you see involves equipment and services that have been created by engineers.

Figure 3 - Golden Gate Bridge, San Francisco[7]

Electrical engineering comprises the largest of all engineering disciplines (25%) and deals primarily with devices that are involved in changing energy from one form to another. Electrical engineers specialize in power transmission, designing and building electricity generators, transformers, and electric motors. They also design radios, televisions, computers, antennas, controllers, and communications equipment. These engineers contributed significantly in developing many of the discoveries connected with electronic equipment, such as computers, telephones, and televisions. A new field within electrical engineering is wireless engineering, which has developed in response to the need for engineers who can work effectively in the mobile world. The computers, phones and other inventions designed by these engineers help us communicate effortlessly with one another irrespective of distances.

Civil engineering is one of the oldest engineering disciplines since it concerns itself with the design and construction of public infrastructure and services. Civil engineers design and supervise the construction of bridges (Figure 3), airports, dams, buildings, canals, and water and sewage systems. In addition, they conduct research to optimize the composition of road surfaces (such as tar, asphalt, etc.), study skyscraper disasters, and work to ensure the structural integrity of buildings. Civil engineering includes specialized areas of practice, such as structural engineering, construction engineering and management, transportation engineering, geotechnical engineering, hydraulic and water resources engineering, and environmental engineering. Buildings, bridges, roads, and other infrastructure designed by these engineers keep us comfortable in our homes and workplaces and help us travel from one part of the country to another quickly and efficiently.

Mechanical engineering is a very broad area of activity that is involved whenever any machinery is being designed and constructed. Mechanical engineers design and manufacture engines, vehicles, machine tools, power plants, consumer items, and systems for heating, air conditioning, and refrigeration. The machines designed by these engineers move and lift loads, transport people and commodities, and produce energy.

Chemical engineering is concerned with the design and operation of processing plants that convert materials from one form to another using chemical processes. These engineers design equipment to process petroleum, coal, ores, corn and/or trees into refined products such as gasoline, heating oil, plastics, pharmaceuticals, and paper. For example, they are responsible for converting crude oil into petrol, kerosene, fertilizers, and many other products that we use every day.

Industrial engineering deals with the efficient, safe, and effective design of plants and offices. These engineers develop, design, install, and operate integrated systems involving people, machinery, and information to produce either goods or services. They are best known for designing and operating the assembly lines that are widely used in manufacturing. We feel the impact of their work when we go to crowded places such as stadiums, but are able to safely and comfortably enjoy watching games alongside thousands of other fans.

Aerospace engineering deals with all aspects of machines that are designed to fly at many different speeds and altitudes, including vehicles that operate in the atmosphere and in space, such as airplanes and space craft. For example, aerospace engineers have designed drone aircraft that fly unmanned missions over hostile territory to drop missiles on targets with pinpoint accuracy, thereby avoiding the need for direct combat operations by troops.

Computer science engineering involves the design and implementation of digital systems and the integration of computer technology into other applications. These engineers design and build computers, network them together, write operating system software, and write application software. For example, the software that was used to write the materials in this text was developed by computer science engineers.

Biochemical engineers combine their knowledge of biological processes with chemical engineering to produce food and pharmaceuticals and to treat wastes. Materials engineers work with different materials such as ores, ceramics, plastics, composites, and metals in order to develop materials that can be used by other engineers. Agricultural engineers help farmers efficiently produce food and fiber. Nuclear engineers design systems that employ nuclear energy. Architectural engineers combine the engineer's knowledge of structures, materials, and acoustics with the architect's knowledge of building esthetics and functionality. Biomedical engineers combine traditional engineering fields with medicine and human physiology to develop prosthetic devices, artificial kidneys, pacemakers, and artificial hearts.

The above fields of engineering are well known for developing products and processes that are used every day by people at home and offices. Frequently, people are not even aware that engineers were involved in the development and construction of the products that they enjoy so much and use constantly.

Engineering technologists bridge the gap between engineers and technicians. Engineering technicians receive a 2-year associate's degree and perform hands-on applications with less emphasis on theory. Finally, craftsmen such as machine shop workers and mechanics, who often receive no formal schooling beyond high school, are generally responsible for transforming engineering ideas into reality. They may work closely with more highly trained engineers to make the engineers' ideas work in the real world[8].

1.3.1   Engineering Societies

Once you leave school and start working in a company or a government agency, you may feel isolated since others in the organization come from other disciplines and you may have fewer opportunities to keep up with new developments in your discipline. You can stay in contact with your discipline and develop a professional network by joining a professional society. The primary function of professional societies is to exchange information between members. This is accomplished by publishing technical journals, holding conferences, maintaining libraries, teaching continuing education courses, and gathering employment statistics. Some professional societies assist members to find jobs or advise the government about the potential impact of new engineering technologies. They may also take a leadership role in defining the future of engineering education as dictated by the needs of industry, the government, and others. In the course of your engineering career, you will probably find it useful to become a member of one or more professional societies. It will be worth your while to get to know these societies and become a member even while you are still in college. This will allow you to become familiar with the valuable services they provide and start to form a professional network even before you graduate.

Table 1 lists the names of some of the major engineering professional societies and their web addresses. Many of the societies promote research and practice in specific fields; others promote engineering profession in general; and others support networks among specific minority groups. Most of the societies hold annual and regional conferences where members can make presentations and interact with other members. In addition, they also publish journals, newsletters, and magazines that inform their members about new research results and help them translate the latest research into new products/services. Most societies are non-profit organizations run by members who volunteer their services for the betterment of the profession.

Many offer inexpensive student memberships so that you can participate and begin to contribute to the profession even while you are still in school.

1.3.2   Professional Registration

In order to protect the public from individuals claiming to be engineers without sufficient credentials, all 50 of the states in the U.S. have passed legislation to register engineers and provide licenses to them. The language and specific provisions of the state engineering licensure laws vary from state to state, but virtually every state law outlines a four-step process under which an applicant who has (1) a four-year engineering degree in a program approved by the state engineering licensure board, (2) four years of qualifying engineering experience, and who successfully completes (3) the eight-hour Fundamentals of Engineering (FE) Examination, and (4) the eight-hour Principles and Practice of Engineering (PE) Examination will be licensed as a professional engineer[9]. Almost all the states now permit engineering graduates to take the first part of the exam covering the fundamentals of engineering at the time of or several months before graduation based on an engineering curriculum approved by the state board. A few states also permit individuals without degrees who have four or more years of engineering experience to take the fundamentals of engineering examination. Passing this exam legally certifies the candidate as an "Engineer-In-Training" (EIT), or an "Engineer-Intern" (EI). Generally four more years of experience are required before the EIT or EI is permitted to sit for the PE exam. Passing the PE exam qualifies the candidate as a licensed professional engineer.

PROFESSIONAL SOCIETIES	WEB ADDRESS
Promoting Specific Fields of Study/ Practice	
Institute of Electrical and Electronics Engineers	www.ieeeusa.org
American Society of Civil Engineers	www.asce.org
American Society of Mechanical Engineers	www.asme.org
American Institute of Chemical Engineers	www.aiche.org
Institute of Industrial Engineers	www.iienet.org
American Institute of Aeronautics and Astronautics	www.aiaa.org
Association for Computing Machinery	www.acm.org
American Society of Environmental Engineers	www.enviro-engrs.org
American Society of Agricultural Engineers	www.asae.org
American Society of Naval Engineers	www.navalengineers.org
American Society of Safety Engineers	www.asse.org
National Institute of Ceramic Engineers	www.acers.org
Society of American Military Engineers	www.same.org
Society of Automotive Engineers	www.sae.org
Society of Manufacturing Engineers	www.sme.org
Society for Mining, Metallurgy, and Exploration	www.smenet.org
Society of Petroleum Engineers	www.spe.org
American Society of Heating, Refrigerating, and Air-Conditioning Engineers	www.ashrae.org
American Nuclear Society	www.ans.org
Minerals, Metals, and Materials Society	www.tms.org

American Academy of Environmental Engineering	www.aaee.net
Promoting Technological Welfare of Nation	
National Academy of Engineering	www.nae.edu
National Society of Professional Engineers	www.nspe.org
American Society for Engineering Education	www.asee.org
Promoting Specific Groups	
National Society of Black Engineers	www.nsbe.org
American Society of Engineers of Indian Origin	www.aseio.org
Society of Hispanic Professional Engineers	www.shpe.org
Society of Women Engineers	www.swe.org

Table 1: Information on Engineering Professional Societies

1.4 Importance of Engineering in the 21st Century

The influence of engineering during the 20th century was profound and this will only increase during the 21st century as engineering innovations are widely applied across national, religious, ethnic, and racial boundaries. The design of a bridge across a river in London, U.K., is very similar to that used in Kolkatta, India or in Manhattan, U.S. They are designed to bear a certain traffic load and as long as that load is not exceeded and it is well maintained, it will serve its purpose well even though it was built in the 1900s. Bridges change peoples' lives by making it possible for them to cross to the other shore of a river in a matter of minutes versus the hours needed when crossing the same stretch of water by swimming or by boat.

Similarly the design of a railway station, space earth station, airport or large automobile plant, whether in South Africa, Chile, India, the U.K., the U.S., or any other country, is very similar. There are only a few global firms that design such structures and there are many similarities among them. It will be to the credit of the engineers working on the projects if the designs change to some extent based on the regional culture and preferences of the local inhabitants. Engineering feats are accepted as a fact of life by a large number of people, as shown in the widespread use of skyscrapers, airports, household machines, and football stadiums. The benefits of engineering are also felt on a humans scale as elderly people use hearing aids, undergo cataract surgery, wear dentures, and use medical procedures that prolong their lives.

People enjoy the products of engineering each day and they are becoming more and more dependent on these products. However, the hazards made possible by engineering are also spreading; a white powder mailed to an address in the U.S. killed several people and closed down the mail operations in major cities for days. There is a strong fear that weapons of mass destruction might be available to leaders of so-called "rogue" nations, who may not hesitate to use them indiscriminately. A bomb, missile, or plane hitting a bridge across the Tigris River in Baghdad, Iraq, or the World Trade Center in New York has the ability to destroy the lives of many citizens who happen to be crossing the bridge or using the building. Even as stem cell research could lead to a cure for many deadly diseases, there is an accompanying fear that it leads to the destruction of embryos.

A stem cell is a primitive type of cell that can be coaxed into developing into most of the 220 types of cells found in the human body (blood cells, heart cells, brain cells, and so on)[10]. Some researchers regard them as offering the greatest potential for the alleviation of human suffering since the development of antibiotics[11]. Over 100 million Americans suffer from diseases that may eventually be treated more effectively with stem cells or even be cured completely. These include heart disease, diabetes, and certain types of cancer.

Stem cells can be extracted from very young human embryos -- typically from surplus frozen embryos left over from in-vitro fertilization procedures at fertility clinics. There are currently about 100,000 surplus embryos in storage. However, a minority of pro-lifers and a majority of pro-life organizations object to the use of embryos. They feel that a few-days-old embryo is a human person. Extracting its stem cells kills the embryo -- an act that they consider murder. Stem cells can now be grown in the laboratory, so (in a pinch) some research can be done using existing stem cells. No further harvesting needs to be performed from embryos. However, the existing stem cell lines are gradually degrading and will soon be useless for research.

Stem cells can also be extracted from adult tissue, without harm to the subject. Unfortunately, they are difficult to remove and are severely limited in quantity. There has been a consensus among researchers that adult stem cells are limited in usefulness -- that they can be used to produce only a few of the 220 types of cells in the human body. However, some evidence is emerging that indicates that adult cells may be more flexible than has previously been believed.

Research using embryo stem cells has been authorized in Britain, but was initially halted in the U.S. by President George W. Bush. He decided on 9th August 2001 to allow research to resume in government labs, but restricted researchers to using only the 72 existing lines of stem cells[12]. By May 2003, most of these lines had already become useless and some of the lines were genetically identical to others; only 11 remained available for research. By May 2005, all were believed to be useless for research. On Sept. 2002, Governor Davis of California signed bill SB 253 into law. This is the first law in the U.S. that permits stem cell research. Davis simultaneously signed a bill that permanently bans all human cloning in the state for reproduction purposes, i.e. any effort to create a cloned individual.

Research continues in U.S. private labs and in both government and private labs in the UK, Japan, France, Australia, and other countries. The Agency for Science, Technology and Research (A*Star) has set aside 70 million Singapore dollars (about U.S.$41 million) to boost stem cell research. According to Channel News Asia reports, the investment will be used over three years to set up the Singapore Stem Cell Consortium, which focuses on applying stem cell research to health care[13].

These inventions and the ensuing policy debates show the strong need for a large number of people of different sexes, races, and religions to become proficient in the engineering profession. In order to participate vigorously in these policy debates and contribute to society, engineers must become more effective communicators, great team players, excellent designers, effective decision-makers, and well-versed in business concepts.

We hope that this textbook, along with the associated multimedia case studies, will give you a clearer picture of what engineers do and how their engineering knowledge, as well as their people skills, will be critical in the future for humanity to live comfortable and good lives. We are pleased that you have chosen to investigate the field of engineering as a possible career option. In the real-world connection below, we provide an excerpt from a book that explains how engineering will become a much more dynamic and important field of study in the near future.

1.5 What do Employers Expect from Engineering Students in the 21st Century?

In order to ensure that engineering students studying in any university in the US receive an appropriate and useful education, a board named the "Accreditation Board for Engineering and Technology, Inc. (ABET)" has been created. It serves the public through the promotion and advancement of education in applied science, computing, engineering and technology and accredits all engineering programs in the U.S. This board goes through an elaborate process to evaluate and accredit colleges and universities in the US that offer programs in engineering. During 2000, this board devised a new set of expectations for the nation's engineering programs (referred to as the ABET a-k criteria) as follows:

Engineering programs must demonstrate that their graduates have:

a) the ability to apply knowledge of mathematics, science, and engineering
b) the ability to design and conduct experiments, as well as to analyze and interpret data
c) the ability to design a system, component, or process to meet desired needs
d) the ability to function on multi-disciplinary teams
e) the ability to identify, formulate, and solve engineering problems
f) an understanding of professional and ethical responsibility
g) the ability to communicate effectively
h) the broad education necessary to understand the impact of engineering solutions in a global and societal context
i) a recognition of the need for and an ability to engage in life-long learning
j) a knowledge of contemporary issues
k) the ability to use the techniques, skills, and modern engineering tools necessary for engineering practice

This expectation is based on elaborate research carried out by ABET together with a number of commercial organizations in order to identify the kind of engineers that are needed for the 21st century. These expectations are further supported by a study performed by researchers at Auburn University. This study asked managers in 23 companies about the skills, knowledge, and abilities that are valued by them in addition to the more traditional skills learned in the major discipline. Table 2 shows the results of this study[14].

Rank of Value-Added Skill, Knowledge, or Ability	Score
1. Better written and oral communication skills	4.62
2. Better developed leadership skills	4.49
3. Improved supervision and management skills	4.13
4. Understand how business decisions affect technical decisions	4.12
5. Working knowledge of project management	4.07
6. Understand how technical decisions affect business decisions	4.04
7. Work in cross-functional teams with other engineering majors	3.85
8. Work in cross-functional teams with business majors	3.73
9. Understand the engineer's role in corporate competitiveness	3.72
10. Internship with a company	3.64
11. Read and understand financial statements	3.46
12. Working knowledge of costing methods and cost accounting	3.41
13. Participate in preparing a business plan for new ventures and products	3.40
14. Working knowledge of enterprise database systems	3.35
15. Working knowledge of concepts such as MRP, ERP and e-commerce	3.34

Items ranked on a scale of 1-5:
1 = Very little value added to the company
2 = Some added value to the company
3 = Good added value to the company
4 = Moderately high added value to the company
5 = Very high added value to the company

Table 2: Skills Valued by Employers of Engineering Students

The ABET requirements and the survey data show that in order for you to be a proficient and effective engineer, you need to acquire skills such as decision-making, team working, communication, ethics, and the ability to work in global businesses in addition to your strong engineering and technical skills.

1.5.1 Leadership and Engineering Competencies

There are several points that students need to remember, as they progress through the coursework in their program of study. As employees (or owners) of organizations, we are not simply required to contribute to the company by sharing our technical skills. Our success depends greatly on our ability as individuals to relate to others, to communicate with others, and to be willing to participate as either leader or follower, depending upon what the situation requires.

This course emphasizes the foundations of engineering that you will need to become a valuable engineering professional. Being a good engineer is not just about building things! Being a good engineer involves having expertise in technical skills, but it also involves being able to work in teams and communicate with others your ideas, designs, or justification for decisions. As a result, this course will focus on a variety of aspects beyond simply learning technical engineering concepts and will help to provide a framework of skills to prepare you to be an effective employee in whatever branch of engineering you choose.

While there will be some activities that enable you to develop expertise in engineering design, there will also be opportunities for you to learn more about yourselves as individuals – for example, you will be able to have a better understanding of your personality and learning style preferences. These assessments will be used to help you learn more about yourselves and your team members.

1.6 Conclusions

The globalization of the world provides opportunities for engineers to become leaders, statesmen, lawyers, doctors, executives, and politicians and guide the destiny of nations. We hope you will include a consideration of the moral consequences of your professional activities in addition to your material and emotional accomplishments and that you will grow into a well-rounded, thoughtful and technically accomplished professional engineer and an influential leader in the 21st century.

---

[1] Lienhard, J. (2000). *The Engines of Our Ingenuity,* Oxford University Press, New York, 2000.

[2] Major portions of this section are extracted from Constable, G. and Somerville B. *A Century of Innovation,* National Academy of Sciences, Joseph Henry Press, Washington DC, 2003.

[3] Lienhard, ibid.

[4] Greatbatch, W., quoted in Constable and Somerville, ibid, p. 189.

[5] Hersey, J., *Hiroshima,* Vantage Books, New York, 1946.

[6] Jackson, J. A., quoted in Constable and Somerville, ibid, p. 225.

[7] http://www.anders.com/pictures/public/05-helicopters/

[8] The material for this section was taken from Holtzapple, M. T. and Reece, W. D., "Concepts in Engineering," McGraw Hill Higher Education, New York, NY 2005.

[9] www.nspe.org, 2005

[10] http://www.religioustolerance.org/res_stem.htm, 2005

[11] http://stemcells.nih.gov/info/faqs.asp#whyuse, 2005

[12] http://www.whitehouse.gov/news/releases/2001/08/20010809-2.html, 2005.

[13] http://news.xinhuanet.com/english/2005-11-01/content_3711082.htm, retrieved on Nov. 2, 2005.

[14] Study done by J. Bryant, Director, Thomas Walter Center, Auburn University, 2001, www.eng.auburn.edu/BET

2 Meeting Today's Challenges with Teams[1]

LEARNING GOALS

- Describe the importance and principles of effective teams in companies
- Define the different kinds of teams that are used in companies
- Describe the benefits of using teams in a technical workplace
- List the characteristics of effective teams
- List the life cycle of the team through the stages of team development
- Identify your individual behavior styles and its impact on team performance
- Show how you could impact team performance
- Learn how to use different tools that can improve team performance
- Actively perform as team using the activities provided at the end of the chapter.

2.1 INTRODUCTION

What is it that today's employers want and expect from graduates of university programs? Is it simply technical expertise? Simply good engineers? Simply good managers? The short answer is no. Deputy Director of the NSF, Joseph Bordogna, states that developing students' communication and leadership skills is critical since in a single project a modern engineer/manager may have to learn how to approach not just a product but finance, safety, environmental, and public policy issues (Codispoti, 1997).

What does that mean for the modern day student? It means a focus on interdisciplinary study and developing the skills of communication, teamwork, as well as understanding the importance of science and math in solving real world problems. In a nutshell, the expectations are that employees will manage tasks well by working effectively with processes and people. The primary goal of the case study approach is to link theory and practice. This creates a more realistic problem to solve, relevant to what really goes on out in the "real world" By analyzing case studies students could obtain the dynamic skill sets applicable to the modern day field of engineering and business.

The current economic landscape requires both the individual and the organization to do more, with less resources and with faster response time. Many

---

[1] This chapter was contributed by Glen B. Olson, MAEd., Learning Unlimited Corp., Tulsa, OK. Part of the research used in this chapter was performed by Vaishnavii Sathiyamoorthy.

factors are forcing organizations to look for new and dynamic ways to meet the demands of the market place. Consider the need for speed, the need to respond to vast technological change and globalization. Most organizations are turning to teams to achieve positive results.

To compete in this environment, the knowledge, skills, experience and perspectives of a wide range of people must be brought together. The days of sitting by yourself in a cubical, cranking it out on a keyboard, working on accounts, or drawing diagrams on a drafting table are gone. Today's projects are multi-dimensional, with obstacles that are multi-faceted involving many different parts of an organization. This requires a coordinated group effort. This group or  "team" creates an environment where participants can keep up with changes, learn more about the business, and gain skills from collaboration.

2.2 DEFINITIONS OF A TEAM

There are numerous definitions of teams, work groups, etc. The categories below will provide clarity when we discuss about various types of groups. Given the task or objective – the type of group may vary. The goal is effective performance and positive results within the given task or process.

Work Group: This is a group for which there is *no significant incremental performance need* or opportunity that would require it to become a team. Such groups tackle different tasks and responsibilities that may or may not be loosely connected.

Pseudo Team: A group for which there could be a significant, incremental performance need or opportunity, but *it has not focused on collective performance and is not really trying to achieve it.* It has no interest in shaping a common purpose or set of performance goals, even though it may call itself a team.

Potential Team: A group for which there is a significant, incremental performance need, and *that is really trying to improve its performance impact.* Typically it requires more clarity about purpose, goals, or work products and more discipline about hammering out a common working approach.

Real Team: A smaller number of people with complimentary skills who are *equally committed to a common purpose, goals and working approach for which they hold themselves mutually accountable.*

16

High Performance Team: A group that meets all the conditions of real teams and has members *who are also deeply committed to one another's personal growth and success.* The high performance team significantly outperforms all other like teams, and outperforms all reasonable expectations given its membership.

Notice what makes a group a real and high performing team. The common thread is the commitment to a common purpose and goals and the use of an approach for which they hold themselves mutually accountable. To achieve high performance, the team members are deeply committed to one another's personal growth and success. In other words, they care about each other.

2.3 THE BENEFITS OF TEAMS IN A TECHNICAL WORKPLACE

The use of teams to impact performance crosses the boundaries of industry and discipline. The evolving market place of doing more with less and at a faster pace has created an environment where two heads are better than one, and three is better than two, and so on. Also the size, complexity and costs of today's engineering and business projects need to be considered. It is impossible to get them done alone.

Teams outperform individuals when:

- The task is complex
- Creativity is needed
- The path forward is unclear
- More efficient use of resources is required
- Fast learning is necessary
- High commitment is required
- The implementation of a plan requires the cooperation of others
- The task or process is cross-functional or interdisciplinary (Scholters 1998)

As you review this list, ask yourself this question: "When do these conditions NOT exist in the modern work place?" Clearly, teams are being utilized because organizations have a need to achieve complex goals faster with fewer resources (physical, technological, financial and people resources).

Historically, engineers and managers have been in control of projects as the result of technical, design, and financial expertise. Consider the construction of the Brooklyn Bridge, which was started in 1868 and completed in 1883. It was a brilliant feat of 19th century engineering. The senior engineer, Washington Roebling, who took over the project after the death of his father John Roebling, guided the completion of one of the most famous bridges in the world, for 11 years, without ever leaving his apartment as the result of illness. Roebling used a telescope to watch the bridge's progress and dictated instructions to his wife who passed on his orders to his workers.

Today, there are many more things to consider, such as, finance, marketing, safety, and environmental issues. Would it be possible for a modern senior engineer to run a project entirely remotely as Roebling did? Not likely. As we think about teams in the engineering world, we are looking at coordinated efforts. Simply sitting at a workstations and designing technically sound projects is only one part of the bigger picture. Albeit a critical piece, it is not the only piece. Successful employees today have to possess the skills and practice to function in a variety of technical and business environments.

It is important to remember that teams are not the solution in every situation. What is important to recognize are the skills needed to participate, contribute and create an effective, high performing team. These are skills that need to be developed and practiced. The structure and delivery of the methodology followed in this book utilizes the case study and team approach to integrate the technical and the people skills required to make the best overall decision. By using the material in this book, you will have an opportunity to develop your technical skills as well as your communication and leadership skills.

2.4 IMPORTANCE OF TEAMS

Teams are important in today's organizations, regardless of industry. The following are some of the demands placed on teams and teamwork.

Organizational Structures: During the past decade, traditional hierarchical structures in organizations have been replaced by team-based structures. This change has increased the demand for team skills and training.

Global Interaction: Technical breakthroughs in communication and travel have reduced the physical distance to an insignificant variable and spawned international teams. This development has imposed new demands on teamwork, which involve multi-cultural and interdisciplinary participants.

Virtual Interaction: Email, the Internet, and Intranets have created new types of teams whose members have little or no face-to-face interaction. This situation has created a demand for hard skills related to the use of technology and soft skills related to interaction in cyberspace.

Changing Workforce: Employees born in the 1970's and raised in a techno environment have lifestyles and work styles different from those people born earlier. Teamwork among members of this generation and between previous generations has created a demand for new structures and methods.

Increased Empowerment: Around the world, citizens want to get involved in the way politicians make decisions in local and national governments, and employees want to get involved in the way managers make decisions in the workplace. New team techniques are required to involve large masses in real-time strategic change.

2.5 CHARACTERISTICS OF HIGH PERFORMING TEAMS

Think back to a time where you were part of a high performance team. What made this team so special? What behaviors did you see demonstrated by team members? What actions did the team and team members do to achieve such a high level of performance? As you think about the list of actions and behavior forms, think of these characteristics as the "answers to the test." The characteristics and behaviors you may have thought of are possibly the ingredients that are common to successful teams.

Your list probably includes such items as: effective leadership, clear goals, clear roles and responsibilities, collaborative problem-solving, shared information, effective communication, clear plans, practice, good attitude of team members, care for each other, good knowledge and skills. The challenge is not in identifying the ingredients, but putting those effective team characteristics into action consistently and intentionally.

No team exists without problems. But some teams – particularly those who have learned to counter negative team dynamics – seem to be especially good at preventing typical group problems. How close a team comes to this ideal depends on the following ten essential ingredients.

2.5.1 Clarity in Team Goals

A team works best when everyone understands its purpose and goals. If there is confusion or disagreement, the team works to resolve the issues.

Ideally, the team:
- Agrees on its charter or mission, or works together to resolve disagreement.
- Sees the charter as workable or, if necessary, narrows the charter to a workable size.
- Has a clear vision and can progress steadily towards its goals.
- Is clear about the larger project goals and about the purpose of individual steps, meetings, discussion, and decisions.

2.5.2 A Work Plan

Work plans help the team determine what advice, assistance, training, materials and other resources it may need. They guide the team in determining schedules and identifying milestones.

Ideally, the team:
- Has created a work plan, revising it as needed.
- Has a flowchart or similar document describing the steps of work.
- Refers to these documents when discussing what directions to take next (its a map!).
- Knows what resources and training are needed throughout the work and plans accordingly.

2.5.3 Clearly Defined Roles

Teams operate most effectively when they tap everyone's talents, and when all members understand their duties and know who is responsible for what issues and tasks.

Ideally, the team:
- Has formally designated roles (all members know what is expected and who does what).
- Understands which roles belong to one person and which are shared, and how the shared roles are switched (for instance, using an agreed upon procedure to rotate the job of meeting facilitator).
- Uses each member's talents, and involves everyone in team activities so no one feels left out or taken advantage of.

2.5.4 Clear Communication

Good discussions depend on how well the information is passed between team members.

Ideally, team members should:
- Speak with clarity and directness.
- Be succinct; avoid using long anecdotes and examples.
- Listen actively; explore rather than debate each speaker's ideas.
- Avoid interrupting and talking when others are speaking.
- Share information on many levels by offering:
  - Sensing statements ("I don't hear any disagreements with John's point. Do we all agree?")
  - Thinking statements ("There seems to be a correlation between the number of errors and the volume of work.")
  - Feeling statements ("I'm disappointed that no one has taken care of this yet.")
  - Statements of intention ("My question was not a criticism. I simply

wanted more information.")

-Statements of action ("Let's run a test on the machine using materials of different thickness.")

Listening

To be an effective listener you should:
- Stay Focused - Keep external distractions to a minimum and work at paying attention to what the other person is saying.
- Receive word and emotions - The words another person uses are only part of the message. Be sure to capture the whole message by also paying attention to the gestures and emotions behind the words.
- Don't interrupt - Interruptions disturb the communication process.
- Resist filtering - try not to judge what the other person is saying based on who that person is or your beliefs about the subject.
- Resist automatic listening - formulating quick responses in your head to what the other person is saying.
- Summarize the message - After you have heard what the other person has said, provide a brief summary to be sure you heard it correctly. Clarify your understanding.
- Focus on understanding not judging.

2.5.5 Beneficial Team Behaviors

Teams should encourage all members to use the skills and practices that make discussions and meetings more effective.

Ideally, team members should:
- Initiate discussions.
- Seek information and opinions.
- Suggest procedures for reaching a goal.
- Clarify or elaborate on ideas.
- Summarize.
- Test for agreement.
- Act as gatekeepers: direct conversational traffic, avoid simultaneous conversations, manage participation, make room for reserved talkers.
- Keep the discussion from digressing.
- Be creative in resolving differences.
- Try to ease tension in the group and work through difficult matters.
- Get the group to agree on standards ("Do we all agree to discuss this for 15 minutes and no more?").
- Refer to documentation and data.
- Praise and correct others with equal fairness, accept both praise and complaints.

2.5.6 Well-defined Decision Procedures

You can tell a lot about how a team is working by watching its decision-making process. A team should always be aware of the different ways it reaches decisions. We will discuss the different methods of decision making in the tool section.

Ideally the team should:

- Discuss how decisions will be made, such as when to take a poll or when to decide by consensus (are there times when a decision by only a few people is acceptable?)
- Explore important issues by polling (each member is asked to vote or state an opinion verbally or in writing)
- Test for agreement ("This seems to be our agreement. Is there anyone who feels unsure about the choice?")
- Use data as a basis of decisions.

2.5.7 Balanced Participation

Since every team member has a stake in the group's achievements, everyone should participate in discussions and decisions, share commitment in the projects success and contribute their talents.

Ideally, the team should:

- Have reasonably balanced participation, with all members contributing to discussions.
- Build on members' natural styles of participation – encourage participation, ask what others need to feel comfortable participating.

2.5.8 Established Ground Rules

Teams invariably establish ground rules (or "norms") for what will and will not be tolerated in the team. We will discuss ground rules in the tool section.

Ideally, the team should:

- Have open discussions regarding ground rules.
- Openly state or acknowledge the norms (write them down).

2.5.9 Awareness of Group Process

Ideally, all team members will be aware of the group process - how the team works together - as well as pay attention to the context of the meeting.

Ideally, team members should:

- Be sensitive and aware of nonverbal communication.
- See, hear, and feel the team dynamics.
- Comment and intervene to correct a group process problem. Ask

questions to check your perceptions.
- Contribute equally to the group process and meeting content.

2.5.10 Use of the Scientific Approach

Teams that use a scientific approach have a much easier time arriving at solutions. Failure to use a scientific approach can lessen the team's chance for success. The scientific approach helps avoid many team problems and disagreements. Many arguments are between individuals with strong opinions. The scientific approach insists that opinions be supported by data.

Ideally, the team should:
- Ask to see data before making decisions and question anyone who tried to act on hunches alone.
- Use basic statistical tools to investigate problems and to gather and analyze data.
- Dig for root causes of problems.
- Seek permanent solutions rather than quick fixes.

2.6 THE GROUP LIFE CYCLE

Think back to the high performing teams you have been a part of – did they start out as high performing? Probably not at first. High performance took the utilization of the actions and behaviors described above, as well as practice, effective leadership, group learning, and time. Remember, we said high performance – NOT perfect performance!

So how does a group of people working together achieve high performance? Is there a secret? In sports you hear of how a team "gels" over time with practice and experience. This process is critical and the steps are almost never skipped. Below is an excerpt from an article by Richard Weber that discusses the process groups go through to reach high performance.

During our professional and social lives, we have all experienced groups that have "gelled" or worked and those that have not. How is it that some groups form and develop from a collection of individuals to a cohesive functional unit (a team)? Is there any predictability in the process or is it just "fate?"

The experience of a "good team" is frequently equated to a mystical experience: something that "just happens," either by divine providence or the match of astrological characteristics, or a blend of individuals' chemistries. Conversely, the experience of a "bad team" is attributed to poor leadership, a lack of compatibility of the members, lack of time, or inattention to process. All of these factors may affect our experiences with teams. Teams are complex living entities, similar in many ways to the individual. Yet few of us think about the development and growth of teams.

In this brief presentation, I wish to share a developmental process that all teams go through. Each team proceeds through three major stages of development, which can be compared to the infant, adolescent, and adult stages of the person. Each stage has four dimensions that need attention: Team Behavior, Team Tasks/Issues, Interpersonal Issues, and Leadership Issues. Numerous behavioral scientists have explored each of these dimensions. I have chosen the work of Bruce W. Tuckman (1965), William Schutz (1971), and Wilfred Bion (1961) for this presentation/exploration.

Each stage is unique in comparison to the other stages and how each team experiences and lives through it. And each stage is lived by all teams that develop into cohesive, functional units. As in the development of the person, certain stages may be more or less pleasant for us to experience. The "stages" must be lived through, however, and each can be treasured as our own unique experience in an inevitable cycle of development.

2.6.1 Stage 1: Infancy ("Forming")

Regardless of what events or structure gives birth to a team, it has to form, to come together. The behaviors in Stage 1 are initially polite and superficial as each person seeks out similarities or common needs. While introductions are made, each individual is testing the amount of compatibility of her or his reasons for being there with the stated reasons of other members. Confusion and anxiety abound as different styles and needs become evident. The goal for the individual is to establish safe patterns for interaction. The team issue is the establishment of basic criteria for membership.

Interpersonally, each individual is working at varying levels of intensity on the issue of inclusion. Some questions raised during Forming are: "Do I wish to be included here and with these people?" "Will they include me, accept me as I am?" "What will be the price and am I willing to pay to be part of this group?" The first stage reflects dependency with regard to leadership. As confusion, ambiguity, and anxiety abound, individuals look to whatever leadership exists in the team or the environment. Whatever direction or information is provided is grasped for guidance. Where there is no

Forming

response from the designated leadership, written descriptions or charges to the team may become a substitute, e.g., The training description says... "If this is also lacking, the absence of direction itself may be brought forward as direction and guidance," or, "As we are getting no direction, we must be expected to proceed ourselves and take responsibility to..." Depending on the similarities in style and needs that exist in the team, and depending on the tolerance for ambiguity that exists in the team, this first stage may be smooth and pleasant or intense and frustrating.

2.6.2 Stage 2: Adolescence ("Storming")

When and if a common level of expectation is developed, the team can then move into the even stormier stage of Adolescence. Possibly the most difficult stage of development to tolerate in either persons or teams, this stage cannot be avoided as it is a crucial stage dealing with power and decision making—necessary skills for the future functioning of the team. In Stage 2, after a base level of expectations and similarities is established, individuals begin to challenge differences in a bid to regain their individuality, power, and influence. Individuals start to respond to the perceived demands of their task, usually with a full range of emotions. Regardless of how clear the task or structure of the team, team members react and will generally attack the designated leadership (facilitators) as well as any emerging leaders within the team. These bids for power and influence may either take the form of direct attacks or covert nonsupport.

Storming

Interpersonally, members are working through their own control needs, both to be in sufficient control and to have some sense of direction. The leadership issue is one of counter dependence, i.e., attempting to resolve the felt dependency of Stage 1 by reacting negatively to any leadership behavior, which is evident. By doing so, members remain dependent in that they are not initiating but reacting. Until individuals break out of this frustrating cycle of reaction and begin initiating independent and interdependent behavior, they will remain in the maze of Stage 2.

As team members persevere in their attempts to create acceptable order/process for decision making within the team, they will lead themselves into Stage 3. The activity and skills gained in this stage are essential for the team to proceed. If the team tries to escape from the unpleasantness of this stage, it will experience failure and will return to Stages 1 and 2 again until the process is completed and power issues identified, including the mechanics of decision making. The more aware the team is of what it has accomplished in this stage, the faster the team will evolve and develop in the future.

2.6.3 Stage 3: Adulthood ("Norming & Performing")

With the frustration of the first two stages behind, the group can finally pull together as a real team, not merely a collection of individuals. Here the team becomes a cohesive unit as it begins to negotiate roles and processes for accomplishing its tasks. Functional relationships are explored and established in spite of differences. The team is ready to tackle its goals by working together collaboratively. With the accomplishment of some goals, team members may gain and share insights into the factors that contribute to or hinder their success.

Norming & Performing

Interpersonally, members are now working out of affection or a caring about others in a deeper, less superficial manner than before. Meaningful functional relationships develop between members. Leadership issues are resolved through interdependent behavior or working with others. Tasks are accomplished by recognizing unique talents in the team -- leading where productive and necessary. As this interplay occurs, trust evolves. The experience of accomplishment, whether it is successfully reaching consensus or solving a team problem provides a powerful unifying force. The sense of "teamness", a feeling of the uniqueness of the team with all its strength and faults, occurs. The team now has an identity of its own that is in no way diminished by it having evolved through the same cycle as countless other teams.

2.6.4 Re-Cycling Through the Process

Teams may proceed through the three stages quickly or slowly, they may fixate at a given stage, or they may move quickly through some and slowly through others. If they do indeed complete all three stages, however, and have sufficient time left in their life together, they will again recycle through the stages. This additional development will lead to deeper insight, accomplishment, and closer relationships.

With the accomplishment of each significant task (or lack thereof), the team must again address the issues of inclusion (What does it mean to be a member now?); control (Who will influence now? How?); and affection (How close and personal can we be? How much can we trust each other?). If the team has learned from its past experience, following cycles will be substantially easier. As in any human development process, the team development cycle has pitfalls. Inattention to possible traps may result in more frustration and anxiety than is needed in the respective stage. If no learning or insight is gained along the way through the cycle, teams will ponder. "Why are we doing or going through all of this again?" Teams must be attentive to their process and learn through it.

Teams may also recycle back to a previous stage before completing the full cycle for a number of reasons:

- Change in the composition of the team (additions or deletions) necessitates returning to Stage 1.
- Change in the charge of the team returns the team back to Stage 1.
- Inattention to the needed activities in a stage will sooner or later require a return to that stage.

2.6.5 Stage 4: Transforming

When the purpose of the team has been achieved, or if the time for the team has expired, the team is faced with transforming. Transforming can take one of two paths: 1. Redefinition - establishment of a new purpose and/or structure; or, 2. Disengagement, Termination, or Death. The team must decide on its future or it will proceed down a frustrating, unfulfilling path. The natural tendency for any team that has successfully achieved a full cycle is to attempt to remain together in some form in the future. The shared experience -- with all of its pain and joy, its meaning and insight -- bonds the members of the team together.

When the purpose has changed or the time has elapsed, however, the team must disengage. Not uncommonly, teams will attempt to define ways of continuing contact after separation through letters or planned reunions in an effort to escape the pain of disengagement. But failure to disengage, to recognize that the life of the team, as its members have experienced it, has come to an end will only lead to greater frustration. However, if members were to remain in contact, or if a reunion were to occur (which seldom happens), the experience will never be the same as the contexts of each of the members will have changed. So as the person must face the inevitability of leaving this life, members must realize that teams too must die. But if nourished, the spirit or experience can live on. Experience the joy of your time together! Complete the cycle! Share good-byes without sorrow! Treasure the uniqueness of your experience! Open yourself to the possibility that having learned here you may facilitate similar experiences elsewhere, equally unique.

2.7 HOW DOES THE INDIVIDUAL IMPACT THE TEAM?

A team is a group of individuals - unique individuals that bring a variety of perspectives, experience, knowledge, skills, and ideas to the group. It is this diversity that can be a great strength or create obstacles to effectiveness. Individual differences are key to the success of your team. Yet these differences can also lead to common workplace issues: stress, conflict, low productivity, ineffective leadership, and resistance to change.

What we say and do – our actions - have a huge impact on teams. Have you ever felt misunderstood? Have you ever had a fierce argument and then wondered what it was all about? Have you ever felt good about how you handled a situation and then later learned that someone didn't like what you said or did? If you answered "yes" to any one of these questions, you will benefit from a study of your own behavior and the behavior of others.

The foundation of personal and professional success lies in not only knowing the technical side of your job, but also in understanding yourself and others, and realizing the impact of your personal behavior on those around you. It is important to recognize that as individuals, we approach situations differently. Without a clear understanding of other team members' needs or expectations, the team or team members may experience ineffectiveness, frustration, or conflict.

The key is to understand that diversity of knowledge, skills, and attitudes can bring advantages and different perspectives. This can also cause disengagement, conflict and a lack of productivity. Said another way, they way you do things can irritate those around you or compliment the process. You may not intend to irritate others, but it happens. In the next section we will discuss the Personal Profile System and other tools you may consider as you form your teams.

2.7 THE TEAM TOOLBOX – RESOURCES TO CREATE HIGH PERFORMING TEAMS

The "Team Toolbox" is intended to provide actual tools that you may find helpful in building an effective team. We have used these materials and tools with many student teams during the case study classes to help form effective teams. What follows is overview of:
- Personal Profile System®
- Group decision-making
- Consensus
- Conducting effective meetings
- Ground rules
- Providing Feedback
- Evaluating Team Performance
- Strategies to Reduce Conflict
- Team building activities.

2.7.1 The Personal Profile System®

So why can't we just understand others? This seems like an easy thing to do. Just sit down and talk about what you need. Experience should tell you it isn't that easy. There are tools that can assist in this process. One such tool that presents the positive contributions of behavior as well as the value and obstacles of homogeny or diversity is called the *Personal Profile System®*. Also know as the DiSC®, the *Personal Profile System®* is currently used in business for the purpose of employee development and team building. The *Personal Profile*

System® is a powerful tool that is easy to understand and simplifies the complexity of human behavior.

The *Personal Profile System®* is based on William Moulton Marston's two-axis, four-dimensional model. This model divides behavior into four distinct dimensions: Dominance, influence, Steadiness, and Conscientiousness (DiSC®).

The DiSC Model of human behavior used in the *Personal Profile System®* was first published in the 1920's by Marston in his book, *Emotions of Normal People*. The title itself gives some insight into the book and into Marston's research focus. Marston, unlike his contemporaries including Freud and Jung, was not interested in pathology or mental illness. He was interested in how normal people felt and behaved as they interacted with the world around them.

Marston's Model is based on two perceptions: the environment as favorable or unfavorable and the person himself or herself as more or less powerful than the environment. An important word in Marston's Model is the word "perception." As modern theorists know, perception of events and circumstances is more important than what those events and circumstances really are, in terms of how people react to them. Perceptions of situations, people, and events determine the reaction to them.

In Marston's Model, an individual perceives his or her environment as either favorable or unfavorable. People who perceive an unfavorable environment see the challenges, the obstacles and the possible pitfalls in the things they undertake. Those who perceive a favorable environment see the fun, warmth among people, and the possible success in the things they undertake. Neither view is more right or more accurate; they are simply different.

The second part of the model is perception of self as more powerful or less powerful than the environment. This is how much impact, control, or effect one believes he or she has on the situation, people and events around him or her. Those people who see themselves as more powerful than their environment believe they can achieve their goals by using their force of will or by persuading others.

Those who see themselves as less powerful than the environment believe they can achieve their goals by consistently cooperating with others or by adhering to established guidelines to ensure quality. Again, neither is more right that the other; they are just different perceptions.

The **DiSC®** provides a common, non-judgmental language for exploring behavioral issues across four primary dimensions:

Dominance: *Direct and Decisive*
D's are strong-willed, strong-minded people who like accepting challenges, taking action and getting immediate results. People with a high D dimension

dominate because they see challenges to overcome and view themselves as more powerful than those challenges. They will try to change, fix or control things.

Influence: *Optimistic and Outgoing*
I's are people-oriented, who like participating on teams, sharing ideas, and energizing and entertaining others. People with a high I dimension try to influence others out of a feeling of being powerful in a favorable environment and wanting others to share their views. They try to influence because they believe they can.

Steadiness: *Sympathetic and Cooperative*
S's are helpful people who like working behind the scenes, performing in consistent and predictable ways, and being good listeners. Those with a high S dimension want to maintain the environment they see as favorable because they see themselves as less powerful than the environment and are, therefore, reluctant to want to try to change things too much. They believe that things are fine as they are and ought to be left alone.

Conscientiousness: *Concerned and Correct*
C's are sticklers for details and quality, like planning ahead, employing systematic approaches, and checking and re-checking for accuracy. Because people with a high C dimension see themselves as having little power in an unfavorable environment, they try to analyze things carefully and then work to achieve high standards or try to follow established rules in order to accomplish their goals.

The *DiSC Personal Profile System®* is available as a resource for any team. There are several versions. We have used the preview, a shorter, non-validated version in many student settings as a starting point for discussion on needs preferences and as a foundation for developing effective communication among teams. It is available at a lower cost and provides an overview of the personalities.

2.8 MAKING GROUP DECISIONS

Decisions are made in a myriad of ways. What follows are some ways decisions are made in teams:

- **The Plop:** Your suggestion is ignored
- **Railroading:** A loud suggestion is acted on without discussion
- **Self-Authorized Decision:** You act immediately on your own suggestion; the group goes along
- **Handclasp:** Quick agreement between two people moves the group to follow their suggestion
- **Voting:** A tally of opinions is taken for and against a suggestion

- **Trading:** "I will agree with you on this one, if you go along with me on the next."
- **Data-Based Decision:** Group or individual moves forward based on input derived mathematically
- **Consensus:** Finding a proposal/solution acceptable enough that all members can support it; no member opposes it. Getting consensus does not mean that everyone must be completely satisfied, or even that it is anyone's first choice

Consensus is a method that encourages participation. It is difficult when decisions need to be made quickly or the team is large. The big advantage is that it gives an opportunity for team members to share their thoughts and perspective. It is important to recognize this is a process that requires attention and facilitation. Consensus does not just happen. Each person must be engaged.

2.8.1 Consensus

Consensus **does not** mean:
- A unanimous vote.
- Everyone getting what they want.
- Everyone finally coming around to the right opinion.

Consensus **does** mean:
- Everyone understands the decision and can explain why it's best.
- Everyone can support the decision.

Consensus **requires:**
- Time – it takes time to get all input and process multiple viewpoints.
- Active participation of all team members – consensus becomes more difficult the larger the group.
- Skills in communication, listening, conflict resolution and facilitation.
- Creative thinking and open-mindedness.

Consensus decision-making is not just a way to reach compromise. It is a search for the best decision through the exploration of the best of everyone's thinking. As more ideas are addressed a synthesis of ideas takes place and the final decision is often better than any single idea that was presented at the beginning.

2.9 CONDUCTING EFFECTIVE MEETINGS

Although individual team members carry out assignments between team meetings, some of the team's work gets done when all the team members are together - during meetings. Productive meetings enhance the chance of having a successful project.

A given is that people are expected to be on time. Otherwise the time of many people is wasted. A meeting should start within a few minutes of the scheduled time, whether all the players are present or not. Once most of the players are present it is time to start.

2.9.1 Use Agendas

Each meeting should have an agenda, preferably one developed prior to the meeting. It should be sent to ALL participants in advance, if possible. If an agenda has not been developed before the meeting, spend the first five minutes of the meeting writing one on a flipchart.

Agendas should include the following information:
- Purpose of the meeting.
- Topics to be discussed and why.
- The lead person for each topic.
- Time estimates.

Agendas usually include the following meeting activities:
- Warm-up - Short activities used to free the mind from outside distractions and get them focused on the meeting
- Agenda review - modify if necessary - have one published before the meeting
- Meeting evaluation

2.9.2 Key Meeting Roles

Meeting Leader or Facilitator

The meeting leader is responsible for keeping the meeting focused and moving smoothly.

Key responsibilities are to:
- Open the meeting
- Review the agenda
- Make sure someone is taking notes and someone is keeping track of time
- Move through the agenda one item at a time
- Keep the group focused on the agenda
- Establish an appropriate pace
- Facilitate discussions through questions
- Encourage participation
- Help team evaluate the meeting
- Gather ideas for next meeting's agenda
- Close the meeting

Timekeeper

The timekeeper helps the group keep track of time during the meeting. This keeps the team from spending all its meeting time on the first few agenda items.

Key responsibilities are to:
- Keep track of the time during meetings.
- Alert the team when the time allocated for an agenda item is almost up so the team can decide whether to continue the discussion, or cut it short, parking lot it, etc. DO NOT simply police the agenda. (e.g. "Time's up. Move on.").

Notetaker

The notetaker records the key topics, main points raised during discussions, decisions made, action items (who will do what by when) and items to be discussed at a future meeting. Notes can be written on standard forms or captured electronically.

Key responsibilities are to:
- Capture the key points for each agenda item.
- Highlight decisions and action items.
- Collect future agenda items.
- See that the minutes are distributed or posted.

Scribe

The scribe posts ideas on a flipchart or whiteboard as the discussion unfolds so everyone can see them. Posting ideas helps the team stay focused on the discussion. It also shows members that their ideas have been captured for consideration, encouraging participation.

Key responsibilities are to:
- Write large enough so all can see.
- Write legibly.
- Check with team for accuracy.

2.10 GROUP PROBLEMS

Regardless of how well we try to manage conflict, sometimes disagreements can become highly emotional. Members polarize; legitimate differences of opinion become win-lose struggles, and progress is stopped. Keep in mind, differences of opinion can inspire and create innovative ideas, the key is awareness and management of the problems or issues.

2.10.1 Sources of Conflict

Most team conflicts relate to one or more of the following, which can be remembered by the word **P R I D E:**

Process - How the team operates on a daily basis

Roles - who does what on the team (lack of clarity)

Interpersonal Issues - How different team members are getting along

Direction - The way the team is proceeding in relation to the common purpose and goals

External Pressures - Considerations such as time, deadlines and resources can have an undue influence on the team

Dealing with Conflict
- Anticipate and prevent problems...Be proactive
- Think of each problem as a group problem
- Neither overreact nor under-react

A leader's range of responses typically includes:
- Do nothing (nonintervention)
- Off-line conversation (minimal intervention)
- Impersonal group time (low intervention - not personal)
- Off-line confrontation (medium intervention more assertive)
- In group confrontation (high intervention - this is to change offensive behavior)
- Expulsion from group...Very last option

Focus on Resolution
- Clarify - Listen and Ask Questions
- Determine points of Agreement and Areas of Difference
- Treat as a Team Opportunity
- Continue Using the Creative Process to Solve

2.11 GUIDELINES TO GROUND RULES

Too often decisions just "happen" in a team; members go along with what they think the group wants. The establishment of ground rules, or "norms," concerning how group processes will be run, how team members will interact and what kind of behavior is acceptable are the foundations for successful teams. Some are stated aloud; others are understood without discussion. Each member is expected to respect these rules, which usually prevents misunderstandings and disagreements. Remember that your team does not operate in a vacuum, with anything else going on; the team is made up of a diverse group of individuals who have many other priorities. It is important to establish expectations and norms that are appropriate to the task. A few of the ground rules to establish are:

Attendance: Teams should place high priority on attending meetings. Identify legitimate reasons for missing a meeting and establish a procedure for informing the group that you will miss a team meeting. Decide how to bring absent team members up to speed.

Promptness: Team meetings should start and end on time. This makes it easier on everyone's schedule and avoids wasting time. How strongly does your team want to enforce this rule? What can you do to encourage promptness? What does "time" mean to your team?

Participation: Everyone's viewpoint is valuable. Therefore, emphasize the importance of both speaking freely and listening actively.

Interruptions: Decide what interruptions your group might face. These might be phone calls (you know we're all mobile), pagers, external conversations with passersby, or internal non-task conversations (socializing). Decide when these will be tolerated and when they won't.

Basic courtesies: Listen attentively and respectfully to others; don't interrupt; hold one conversation at a time; and so forth.

Assignments: Much of the team's work is done between meetings. When members are assigned responsibilities, it is important they complete their tasks on time. Commit to this!

Breaks: Yes, breaks! Decide whether and under what circumstances smoking will be allowed, whether to take breaks, break frequency, and how break length.

Rotation: Your roles and duties will change as part of the work situations and projects you are involved in. Be sure to plan the rotation of members and roles.

Responsibilities: Up-front (no surprises) and assist each other in the clarification of these roles. Remember to use the behavior style survey information as a reference tool.

Meeting place and time: Specify a regular meeting time and place, establish a procedure to notify and remind attendees of meetings. Make it a logical place where distractions are minimal!

2.12 FEEDBACK

There are two types of Feedback. The first type of feedback comes when the team meetings take place. The second type of feedback comes when the project is over, the facilitative team leader or the manager of the team must give feedback about the team's performance in the particular project and what they where able achieve through this project. This feedback may be positive or negative. But this feedback is very important to maintain the health of the team.

Feedback is a very important part of team meetings. It should be constructive. When you speak in a meeting on a common problem, just state the facts without any exaggeration, attribution or motives. Try to express about what you feel about the whole issue and how others behavior affects you. Now explain the facts that you have observed and justify your viewpoint.

Clearly describe the changes you expect from the team. Try to make the other member understand that the solution provided by you will help them solve the problem. Now let the other members respond to your ideas and speak about what they feel about the problem and discuss the fact so that the team will be able to reach a consensus on a solution. Thus feedback is playing a major role in any team meeting from the beginning. Therefore, while giving your feedback in a team meeting:

- You have to be conscious of the word you use
- Your temper has to be stabilized
- You have to listen to other members patiently
- You have to concentrate on the whole issue clearly
- You have to analyze the issue before giving the feedback to the other members of the team

2.13 EVALUATING TEAM PERFORMANCE

Evaluating team performance is essential for an organization, which has teams working on it. Every organization invests a large sum of money and time in organizing and training teams, so the managers will have to know whether the teams function effectively or not. Generally this evaluation helps the management to enhance their performance. One main approach to evaluate team is to examine the team's health by assessing its activities and structure.

In order to evaluate the team's health, let's take the stages of team development into consideration. Since these stages undergo a variety of predictable phases over a period of time, it will give you a clear picture of the team's performance. A health chart can be prepared in each stage to evaluate the health of their team, provided the team members and team leaders have to know what a health chart is? Or how to respond to it?

2.13.1 Health chart for orientation stage (forming)

This stage can also be considered as the start-up phase. The manager will have to check if the following list of things is going on well in their concerned team.

Mission statement	Yes	No
Boundaries defined	Yes	No
Training defined	Yes	No
Formational meeting	Yes	No
Meeting room available	Yes	No
Situation appraisal	Yes	No

2.13.2 Health chart for conflict and cohesion stage (storming and norming)

This stage is for the manager to evaluate if the team meets regularly and if the attendance is adequate in the meeting. This stage can also be called as testing phase. If it meets, how well they contribute to the decisions taken in the meetings? These are the some of the facts to clearly concentrate to analyze the performance level of the team.

Regular meetings	Yes	No
Consensus decision making	Yes	No
Performance indicator used	Yes	No

Attendance	High	Medium	Low
Dysfunctional behaviors	High	Medium	Low
Emotional bank accounts	High	Medium	Low

2.13.3 Health chart of task-performance phase

This stage is also called as *performance phase.* The managers should check on a number of team behaviors and attributes in order to keep the team healthy. The manager must keep in track of certain things like, if the team meets regularly? Is management reviewing the team's activity? Are dysfunctional behaviors emerging? These are the facts to be keenly noticed by the manager to evaluate the team.

Regular meetings	Yes	No

Progress reviewed by management	Yes	No
Success recognized	Yes	No
Members satisfaction	Yes	No

Attendance	High	Medium	Low
Dysfunctional behaviors	High	Medium	Low

These understanding through the charts will help the team leader and the members know what has been the performance level of the team. Now the overall picture of the team will help the facilitative team leader or the manager to determine if bringing in new leadership can invigorate the team. Has the team fallen into a pattern of dysfunctional behavior? Is there a need to formally close the team? All this can be cleared in understanding another chart, which is a *Re-testing or Closeout phase,* occurs during the adjourning stage.

2.13.4 Health chart for Dissolution phase (Adjourning)

New Leadership needed?	Yes	No
New situation appraisal needed?	Yes	No
Closure needed?	Yes	No

It is important to understand the health of the team to evaluate the effectiveness of the team. An unhealthy team can hardly function effectively. However the manager should always keep an eye on the bottom line indicators of success, such as costs, quality, volume of output, and meeting schedule.

2.13.5 Strategies to Reduce Conflict

Conflict is one of the major issues in any team environment. Groups often have a difficult time acknowledging and resolving conflicts. If the relationship is better among group members, there is more pressure to avoid or minimize conflict. Resolving conflicts within the teams or between teams has become one of the major challenges for many organizations.

Conflict is normal to occur in an organization's work setting. Your interests may differ from the interests of other members working with you, and these differences may cause conflict. The trick is not to avoid conflict but to know how to resolve conflict effectively to accomplish the tasks of the team and still maintain the health of the team.

Normally, conflicts that could occur in a team include issues like vacation timings for different members, who will work in bad weather, or in the budget proposal of the company for purchasing tools. Some conflict may occur between your team and others. The conflict starts in any team when you try to understand what your interests are and what the interests of others may be. *The best way to resolve difference is to understand everyone's interests, talk about them, and find the best way to meet everyone's needs (Fisher 1980).*

In order to solve the problem of conflict is it also important for us to understand the different characters of different people working in the team. Attributes like their personality, the dominant nature that influences his or her behavior, for which the DiSC personal profile preview is giving a vast explanation about different characters and their performance level in a team.

For instance, how would you work in a team environment? What would be your reaction to the issues that will come up in a corporate environment? Every team member should know what is his tolerance level is. Once you know what your personality type, what you expect out your co-worker and the management, and then you would try to take things without much friction. Hence, conflict is an important factor that has to be taken care of, in a team from the beginning.

2.14 TEAMBUILDING ACTIVITIES

Provided in this section are teambuilding activities that can be used with students. These activities are fun and provide ways for the students to get to know each other and familiarize themselves with the basic skills of collaborative problem solving before being separated into project teams and starting to work on course content.

We have used these activities with a variety of students, most specifically, engineering and business students in the case study curriculum at Auburn University. We have also used them with pharmacy students at Samford University, and Blount Scholarship students at the University of Alabama.

These are intended to be a resource to discuss and practice the skills demonstrated by high performing teams. It is worthwhile discussing topics about teams and then practice using the activities so the groups can analyze their behavior and performance as a group, rather than focus on engineering or business content. It also initiates the "forming" process of the group life cycle.

2.14.1 Categories

PROPS: 1 (one only) SIZE: 10-100

SPACE: Large area (In or Out) ORIGIN: Karl Rohnke

TIME: 15-30 minutes

INTENT: To find commonalties and to get to know each other better.

ACTION: People get together in common categories and then chat.

HIGHLIGHTS: This is a great activity for soon after group arrival.

PREPARATION: You will need a whistle for large very noisy groups. You really don't care what groups form under a category, just that people are invited to join a group and have a mutual discussion.

SCRIPT: This game is about incorporating yourself into a common group and having a short conversation with people you meet there. You may not finish your conversation in the time we have, but these are conversation starters, which I hope you'll pick up on later.

In a minute, I'll call out a category like SIBLINGS and you'll have to recall how many of those you have and find everyone else who has the same number as you (Zero can be a group). Or I might call out "Sock Color" and you'll need to get in the group where everyone has the same color socks as you (None can be a group).

Once you find your correct membership have a conversation about yourselves. Start with the reason you are there such as what it was like as an only child or why you choose not to wear socks. Then move on to find other things you might have in common with folks. After a while, I'll blow the whistle. We'll see who is in which groups and then we'll try another category. Any questions? GO!

VARIATIONS: Ask everyone for their category ideas. Here are some suggestions (remember "none" and "don't know" can be a group).
- Wearing: the same jewelry, type of shoes, color of pants / shirt.
- Having: the same hair style / length, or color of eyes / hair / nails.
- Owning: the same kind of pet, car, computer, cell phone, pager.
- Number: of bedrooms / toilets in your home, kids in your family.
- Time of the day: that you exercise, shower / bathe, read the paper.
- Favorite: type of food, drink, books, movies, music, exercise

2.14.2 Entrapment

OBJECTIVE: Place loaded traps in a circle as quickly as possible so that they are positioned like dominoes.

INSTRUCTIONS: You will need 4-20 mousetraps. Ask the group to plan for 5 minutes to set and place all the mousetraps so that they overlap each other as shown in the picture. No one can touch a trap until the planning time is over.

When a trap is touched the timer starts, when the last trap is placed in position and no one is touching any, the timer stops. (Current fastest time for 15 traps is 1 minute 5 seconds.)

VARIATIONS: Don't make it a timed event. Just let people position the traps. When the traps are successfully placed, get a Ping-Pong ball and take turns bouncing it inside the circle and to another person until the traps go off. If it is too easy to do one bounce in the circle, challenge them to make the ball bounce twice before the next person catches it.

2.14.3 Paper Chute

PROPS: 4 sheets of paper, Tape, 4 paper clips, Scissors (optional), Felt tip markers (optional), Stop watch for the facilitator or timer

OBJECTIVE: Design a structure that will free-fall as slowly as possible.

INSTRUCTIONS: Construct a contraption that, when dropped 8 feet, will take the longest time to reach the ground. It must free-fall and be self-contained (no strings or other aids attached). You may only use the materials provided. You will have three drops to get the best time. You can drop the same thing all three times or you can use up to three different designs. The person timing your drop will count down, 3, 2, 1, drop! The dropper will need to let go of the apparatus on drop. The timer will start when you let go and will stop when the apparatus first touches the floor.

FACILITATOR NOTES: If you have the time, try a best time out of three drops. It gives everyone a chance to make the best of a sophisticated falling device. When people start attempting to defy gravity they may ask very specific questions about the instructions. Here are some of the answers I often give: 1) you cannot bring in any extra materials, but you do not have to use all the materials. 2) No, you cannot lie on the floor and blow air to keep the object up longer; it is a free-fall. 3) Someone from your team can drop the creation, however, it must be dropped, not thrown.

Just in case you were wondering how fast an object might fall without any air resistance: (x seconds)2 = (distance falling)/(.5 x 9.8 m/s2). For 8 feet (2.44 meters) the fastest free-fall is .71 seconds. A personal best on this activity is 4.88 seconds. No tricks, no kidding.

VARIATIONS: Consider prizes or recognition to the device that is most esthetically pleasing or the most interesting. Let people decorate their "thing" and market it to the group. Another variation requires that each team use all the materials you provide.

2.14.4 Water Towers

PROPS: For each team of 4-6 people: 12 ounce (340 g), package of spaghetti per team, 1 water balloon approximately 4 inches (10 cm) in diameter, 1 roll of masking tape

OBJECTIVE: Build a water tower as high as possible out of spaghetti and tape.

PREPARATION: Carefully fill a balloon with water until it is approximately 4 inches in diameter. Place the props on the floor or on tables so that each team will have plenty of room to begin construction.

INSTRUCTIONS: Using only the supplies provided, build the tallest, free-standing, self supporting tower that will support the water balloon at the top. You will have 20 – 35 (you select what works for your situation) minutes to complete the task.

SCENARIO: Many people are unaware that in this part of the country fresh water can be very hard to come by. The water that is available has to be pumped up several hundred feet from the Ersatz Aquifer. Knowing that you all would be here to work on building teams, the "locals" have asked us for your help to design a new water tower for the area. They want us to build a model that meets their building requirements. The tower needs to be as tall as possible to increase the water pressure in the pipes. The model that we are building can use only 12 ounces of dry spaghetti and one roll of masking tape as building materials. The tower must be free-standing and self-supporting. Finally, the tower must support the water for which it is being built. (Show a water balloon.) Great rewards will be given to the team that builds the tallest tower that meets the requirements above. You have 35 minutes to build the tower. Go!!!

FACILITATOR NOTES: When we started using these materials for teams to build towers we used only masking tape and spaghetti. The towers would go higher and higher, but rarely, after the time expired, did a tower stand more than 18 inches. It seems that most people built their structures for quick height and little stability. As a result, most towers crumbled to the floor before the end of the activity.

We added the water balloon to the supplies to add an extra challenge. It was interesting to discover how differently each small group approached the task. The weight of the balloon caused them to focus on the strength of the structure as well as its height. As a result, every tower stood and was over 3 feet tall! The same dynamic has occurred with subsequent teams. Given a greater challenge, each team created greater results with the same building materials.

2.14.5 Balloon Castles

TIME: 30 min. - 1 hour

PROPS: Two rolls of transparent tape & 100 balloons for each team of 5-12 people.

OBJECTIVE: Build the tallest free-standing, self-supporting balloon structure possible in 20 minutes.

PREPARATION: Set out 2 rolls of tape in dispensers and count 100 balloons for each team. Be sure to select a space where the ceiling is high enough to accommodate a tall structure.

OBSERVATIONS: It is really interesting to watch teams plan and do this activity. The vision of the finished product is often much different from the actual. Many teams jump right in to the solutions and waste time later trying to define the structure and how to organize it. Some of the most effective teams take a designated time up front to decide a plan, make role assignments, and come up with one or two contingencies before they get busy. Too often teams set lofty goals and forget that a solid foundation is required or the whole thing will tumble to the floor.

Discoveries about balloons and transparent tape are fun to watch. One common strategy is to blow the balloons to full capacity since each one is taller that way...until they break! Another common design strategy is to build layers that will fit like a puzzle upon the lower layers...too bad the balloons are not a uniform size and shape when they are inflated. The tape causes its own problems since transparent tape can form sharp points that only burst the most critical balloons. The tape can also make one heck of a mess if the participants are not careful where it sticks.

REFERENCES

Bion, W.R. Experiences in Teams, New York; Basic Books, 1961

Jon R. Katzenbach and Douglas K. Smith, The Wisdom of Teams: Creating the High-Performance Organization © 1993

Scholters, Joiner and Barbara J. Streibel, The Team Handbook, Second Edition Oriel Incorporated, 1998.

Schutz, W.C. Here Comes Everybody, New York; Harper & Row, 1971

Sivasailam Thiagarajan and Glen Parker, Teamwork and Teamplay: Games and Activities for Building and
Training Teams, Pfeiffer/Jossey-Bass, 1999.

Tuckman, B.W. Development Sequence in Small Teams. Psychological Bulletin 1965, 63, 284-399.

Weber, Richard C. "The Group: A Cycle from Birth to Death." Reading Book for Human Relations Training. NTL Institute, 1982.

SOURCE BOOKS FOR THE ACTIVITIES

Sikes, Sam, Feeding the Zircon Gorilla, 1995

Sikes, Sam, Executive Marbles, 1998

Evans, Priest, Sikes, 99 of the Best Corporate Games We Know, 2000

ABOUT THE AUTHOR

Glen B. Olson, MAEd., Partner – Learning Unlimited Corp. With four years of corporate training experience as a Regional Training Manager with Kinko's Inc., Glen has trained a variety of topics such as; leadership development, technical training, customer service training, team building and conflict resolution to a variety of executive and front line groups. He has incorporated experiential processes into these diverse training sessions. Glen holds a BA in History from Auburn University and a Master's degree in Curriculum and Instruction from Virginia Tech. Glen brings high energy and enthusiasm to all programs and processes.

Learning Unlimited is an innovative leader in the development and delivery of experiential training programs worldwide. Learning Unlimited offers a wide variety of Leadership Development programs using reliable, valid and proven approaches to adult learning. Their experiential programs place people in structured environments designed to accurately reflect situations in the workplace. The decisions participants make during the experience determines the outcome. This powerful "learning laboratory" provides the opportunity to practice new leadership behaviors. There are multiple facets to Learning Unlimited's products and services including: Structured Training, Meeting Events/Conferences, Leadership Development, Team Building, Train the Trainer programs, and Training Resources. Find them on the web at: **www.learningunlimited.com**

3 Engineering Workplace Communication: Presentation and Writing[1]

Learning Goals

- Give examples of the types of situations requiring engineers to communicate
- Understand the ideas key to effective engineering communication
- Emphasize how professional success depends on the effectiveness of communication

3.1 INTRODUCTION

- Two engineers are discussing a technical problem over coffee in the cafeteria. One of them draws a rough diagram on a napkin, and the other suggests modifications in the diagram. When they go back to their offices, one of the engineers takes the napkin in order to preserve the diagram.
- An engineer meets with the vice presidents of two divisions, along with a representative from finance. The meeting is in the office of one of the vice presidents. The vice presidents are deciding whether to go ahead with a product launch, which the engineer favors. The engineer describes the product, outlines arguments for launch, and answers questions.
- A staff is meeting to discuss the costs and benefits of a system modification. The group includes representatives from manufacturing, marketing, sales, and engineering. During the meeting, the engineer explains potential modifications, using prepared slides that include words, drawings and diagrams. The engineer answers questions from others, using the whiteboard to illustrate and explain points.
- An engineer is preparing a technical report on the cause of malfunctions in a manufacturing process. The report covers both technical issues and management implications. Readers will include other engineers and managers. The writer must decide how to use diagrams, equations, and engineering terminology in combination with

---

[1] This chapter was developed by Judith Shaul Norback, Joel S. Sokol, Peter J. McGuire, and Garlie A. Forehand, Georgia Institute of Technology, GA.

47

non-technical terminology so that all readers will understand the important issues.

Each of these vignettes is an example of **workplace communication by engineers**. The instances illustrate the wide range of communication events that are part of a practicing engineer's professional life. They range from highly informal to highly formal. The audience might be one person or many. The language might be technical or non-technical. The format might be oral, written, or a combination of the two. The situations described share an important characteristic: **the engineer's professional success depends on the effectiveness of the communication.**

What makes communication so important to professional engineers? Communication is the way that engineers get their ideas implemented. It is almost always true that engineers' work has an impact through the work of others. Effective communication improves an engineer's value as a team member, and opens up opportunities for career advancement.

The examples illustrate some key facts:
1. Communication is a necessary aspect of all of the work of professional engineers.
2. Engineers communicate professionally with colleagues and clients who have diverse organizational roles and educational backgrounds.
3. Without good communication, even the best engineer's technical recommendations will not be implemented.

Practicing engineers, engineering supervisors, and senior executives all report that communication skills are critical to an engineer's career. Yet, most people are familiar with the stereotype of engineers as good at analyzing and calculating but bad at communication. Probably the most important reason for this stereotype is that engineering students get little training in communication. So, how does a student prepare for the communication demands of an engineering career? This chapter includes some concepts and strategies that will be helpful.

In this chapter, we will outline basic principles that can be applied to all workplace communications. An engineer who integrates these principles into day-to-day professional work will be well equipped to handle diverse communication events. After outlining the basic principles, we will show how to apply them to important communication tasks that confront all engineers: oral presentations and written reports.

The suggestions in this chapter came from engineering workplaces. They were made by professional engineers, supervisors, and senior executives during interviews that were part of research on engineering communication.

3.2 Characteristics of Engineering Communication

The engineer communicates professionally with a wide range of people. Some communication partners are fellow engineers with similar vocabulary and professional perspectives. Others include supervisors, corporate executives, workers and customers.

Communication is often very different in engineering than in other aspects of life. The purpose of engineering communication is to explain a technical idea or analysis. As we explain later in this chapter, the way you explain should vary according to your audience – for example, a fellow engineer might want to see all of the equations that describe the physical stresses on a bridge, while a city planner (who doesn't have an engineering degree) might be more interested in the effect your new bridge would have on traffic flow. However, regardless of the audience, there are several important characteristics of engineering communication that can differ from what you encounter in other aspects of life, or even in other courses you take.

Engineering communication should be clear and simple: Unlike literature and poetry, where complex sentence structure and flowery metaphors are often highly valued, the purpose of engineering communication is to get as much of your audience as possible to understand your ideas. Therefore, you should present things as clearly and simply as possible.

Engineering communication should be short and to the point: Many people enjoy good, long movies or books, but very few people read engineering reports for fun. Most people you will communicate with will be hearing or reading your communication as part of their busy workday, and they will appreciate your ability to explain things clearly without taking too much of their time.

Engineering communication should be precise and accurate: Imprecise statements are common in non-engineering settings – for example, a politician might say, "My health care plan will cover a lot more Americans." However, engineers are expected to be more precise when communicating. "This circuit will operate 5 times faster" gives more useful information than "this circuit will operate a lot faster."

Engineering communication should never be misleading: Engineering is different from advertising. Even when you are trying to influence their decision-making, the people you communicate with will trust that you are giving a truthful (and not misleading) representation of the facts. To find out more about what behavior is expected of engineers, read the Code of Ethics for Engineers (published by the National Society of Professional Engineers) and discussed in the engineering ethics chapter.

Engineering communication should not have a surprise ending: The punch line of a joke and the final clue of a murder mystery are enjoyable because there are surprise endings. We never know what to expect until it happens. Engineering communications are different. They are meant to explain, not entertain, so it is important to give your audience information up front. Otherwise, they might lose interest. Professionals in the workplace stress the importance of stating the recommendations at the beginning of the communication.

The characteristics of engineering communication described above included: a) the communication should be clear and simple, b) it should be short and to the point, c) the communication should be precise and accurate, d) it should never be misleading, and e) it should not have a surprise ending.

The previous paragraphs have described how engineering communication differs from communication in other aspects of life. On the other hand, many general characteristics of good communication also apply in engineering. For example, engineers are expected to communicate using correct grammar and spelling. We assume that you have already learned things like this, so our focus in this chapter is on engineering-related aspects of communication.

In later sections of this chapter we will offer specific suggestions for applying principles of communication in oral presentations and written reports. Next we will review the elements of communication. Audience characteristics will be covered as well as the form of a communication – the medium or the method used to convey information and the type of document involved. Next organizational context, or the language and traditions of an organization, will be described. Finally, the content of the communication – the information contained in the message – will be covered.

3.3 Elements of Communication

Suppose you are a professional engineer with the need to communicate a particular message to a group of significant individuals. Figure 4 can be used to identify the elements that you need to plan and implement your communication.

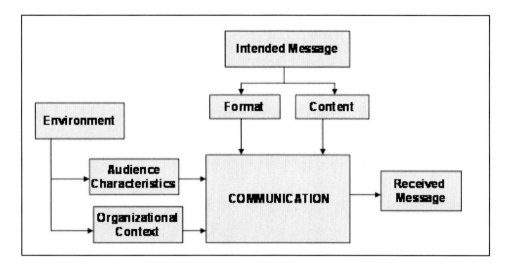

Figure 4: Elements of Communication

3.3.1 Audience Characteristics

It is tempting to believe that our job as communicators is to construct a message that is technically accurate, logically reasoned, and grammatically correct. The fact is, however, unless the audience understands the message, the communication is unsuccessful. In order to communicate in a way that will be understood, we need to recognize what our audience is like. Analysis of the audience is an indispensable part of communicating.

- A key characteristic of audience members is their **educational and professional background**. Some audience members may have an engineering background and will be prepared to understand a technical point that you wish to make. Sometimes, however, your audience will include persons with different technical backgrounds and others with no technical background.

- Second, audience members differ in the **kinds of information they need**. For example, colleagues with whom you are discussing the design of a new airplane wing need to see detailed equations and test results to appreciate your ideas. On the other hand, detailed technical analysis is less important if the audience members only need to understand the impact that the decision will have on the wing manufacturing processes.

- Third, audience members also differ in the **roles** they play in the decision-making process. Some audience members might be influential decision-makers who will have considerable impact on whether your ideas are implemented or not. Influential roles include executive decision-making, financing, and marketing.

3.3.2 Form

The form of a communication includes the medium used and the type of document involved. The **medium** of a communication is the method a person uses to convey information. Some examples include email, fax, phone, and oral communication. A communication always takes place via one or more media, and the medium itself affects how the message is received. For example, a face-to-face presentation is more interactive than a written report. The writer of a report must imagine questions and objections that would come to the surface in a meeting.

A communicator must also make decisions about the type of document to use to convey a message. Common engineering documents include technical reports, progress reports, memos, slide presentations, and user manuals. Each of these styles has its own rules and formats. For example, readers of technical reports expect particular features such as standardized charts and tables. In many organizations, executive summaries are expected for all documents. An executive summary states the main ideas and summarizes the support in a page or two. Preparation of an executive summary is an important skill in its own right. Some managers will read only the executive summary, and others in the organization will often act on the material in the executive summary rather than reading the larger document. Therefore, the executive summary should be a self-contained mini-report rather than an "advertisement" for the full version.

3.3.3 Organizational Context

Each organization has its own language and traditions. Practicing engineers report consistently that successful communicators learn the organizational context and history and take it into account in communication. Successful communicators are sensitive to **"what things**

mean around here." For example, at a home improvement store the sales clerks on the floor are called "aprons." In a bank, a credit problem in an automobile portfolio, for example, is referred to as a "rock." People say, "We're chipping away at the rock."

3.3.4 Content

When one sets out to communicate there is a message that the communicator wants to transmit. In fact, the message that is received might not be the same message the sender had in mind. The effective communicator works hard to formulate a message that will not be misunderstood. Knowledge of audience, form, and organizational context are important considerations when creating effective and influential messages. The messages must also be clear and concise.

As shown in Figure 6, all four of these elements of communication contribute to the message that is received by the audience.

In the remainder of this chapter, we will apply these ideas – the characteristics and elements of communication – to improving communication. We will consider two frequently encountered types of communication: oral presentation and written reports.

Scenario

Suppose you are an engineer working as a consultant for a hospital planning an expanded emergency room (ER). The hospital needs the expansion because patients who need to get into the ER have a very long wait. In making recommendations you have taken into account the cost and placement of the required medical instruments and technology. You have considered how to prioritize the patients' conditions once they enter the waiting room. You have studied how to optimize moving ER patients into hospital beds. In five days you'll be presenting the recommendations to your audience. After the presentation, you will be expected to submit a report detailing and justifying your recommendations.

3.4 The Communication

Think about the communication steps in front of you. How should you go about 1) preparing for the communication, 2) delivering it, and 3) following up after the communication? These steps are illustrated in Figure 5 and discussed below.

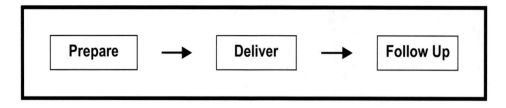

Figure 5: Process of Communication

3.4.1 Preparation

To prepare both the oral presentation and the written report it is necessary to first plan a communication strategy and create the material necessary for it (Figure 6). As part of planning your communication strategy we will discuss how to identify the purpose of the communication, learn the characteristics of the audience, and select an appropriate medium and type of document for your communication.

Next, as part of creating the material for the communication we will review how to plan the logical sequence of material, support the conclusions, prepare materials that are clear, and check the content of the material.

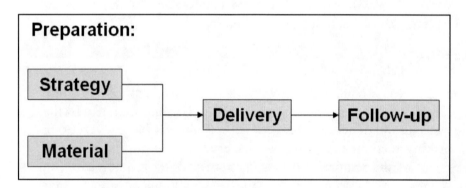

Figure 6: Preparation, Delivery, and Follow-up

3.4.1.1 Strategy

Identifying a communication strategy is the first step in preparing a communication. To develop an effective strategy, it is important to take into account the purpose of the communication, the audience, and the material used (Figure 7).

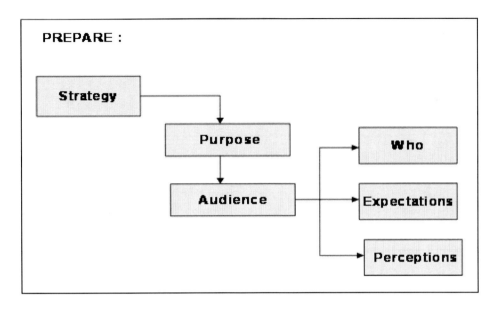

Figure 7: Purpose and the Audience

Purpose

The **purpose** might be one of the following:

- Decision-making: the audience will use the information you communicate to decide whether or not to pursue a course of action, or to select the best of several alternatives. This is the purpose of your oral presentation in the hospital ER scenario. When communicating in a decision-making situation, it is important to describe the decision to be made along with any alternative approaches. Then describe what will happen if each approach is chosen. Finally, give your recommendation and explain why you believe it to be the best alternative. Remember that one of the characteristics of engineering communication is that you are trusted to give your true opinion and to support it with technical analysis. In this case, you should give your recommendation about how the ER should be expanded and why it will operate more effectively.

- An update on a project: the audience will use the information you communicate to assess your progress, either from a technical or non-technical perspective. If this is the purpose of your communication, include the main goals of the project, describe your progress toward each of the goals, and indicate your next steps toward project completion. It is also important to describe honestly any difficulties you have encountered or expect to encounter. In the best case, your audience members might be able to offer a helpful suggestion ("have you tried a fast Fourier transform [a method to analyze functions]?"). At worst, you can keep their expectations to a realistic level; if the project fails – and many do, no matter how good an engineer you are.

- Introducing your audience to a new issue: from your communication, the audience will gain a new understanding about the topic at hand. "Issue" might refer to something either technical (like a new process for extracting chemicals) or non-technical (like the need for a better satellite antenna design). In either case, describe the issue and its background. Include examples to illustrate the issue and then give reasons the audience needs to be aware of the issue.

Both oral and written communication requires careful identification of purpose. Of course, there are some purposes that are especially well served by written reports. Examples are documenting the steps of a project, presenting the technical explanation behind a recommendation, and creating a record that can be consulted in the future. On the other hand, some purposes, such as project updates for high-level executives, are better served by oral reports. The key is to identify purposes explicitly, and make sure that each part of the communication contributes to fulfilling a purpose.

In the hospital scenario, there are two main purposes. One is to present a recommendation from among several alternatives, and allow hospital executives to ask questions about each. The presentation should not get bogged down in detail, but should instead give a brief overview of the various alternatives and the reasoning behind your recommended choice.

The other main purpose is to create a record that can be reviewed as the decision is being made so the hospital president can determine quickly what is being recommended and why. The body of the report should provide more detail than the presentation covered. For example, document how the alternative approaches were identified and the reasons for the recommendation. Include detailed data in the appendices.

Audience

We have just discussed the first part of the communication strategy, identifying the purpose of the communication. The second part of selecting a strategy is gathering information about the people who will be receiving the communication. You will need to identify who will be in your audience (and how their backgrounds will affect their ability to understand your communication), what they expect to get out of your communication, and what their perceptions of the main issues are.

Who is the audience?

If the communication is a face-to-face presentation, it might be possible to identify exactly who will be in the audience. Before arriving at a meeting, an effective communicator will learn the names of audience members, their positions, and how they fit into the project team. Will senior management be at your talk? Will your engineering supervisor be there? What about line workers? Knowledge of audience characteristics will help you decide what information to include in your talk and how much detail to give. For instance, with a Chief Executive Officer (CEO) or an Executive Vice President in the audience, you will want to stress the major points without going into a lot of detail. Senior executives expect to be told what the big-picture issue or problem is at the beginning of the presentation. Then they want to know potential solutions and recommended action steps. Very little low-level detail is required. In contrast, if you present a change in procedure to assembly line workers you will need to describe their new procedure in more detail and highlight changes they will experience, instead of giving a complex overview of the situation.

The audience for a written report is harder to pin down. You will probably not know all of the specific persons who will read and act on your report. Analysis of the audience, however, is just as important for a written report as for a face-to-face presentation. Who will read the report? What will they expect to learn? What background will they bring to the communication? What roles will they play in implementing the recommendations? You should know the answers to these questions so you can write the report in a way that your audience will be interested in reading it.

What do audience members expect?

Whether preparing oral or written communication, it is necessary to assess audience expectations. Often, you will know who some of the most important recipients of your communication are. The person who asked for your report will be a key audience member. It is important to check whether internal or external experts will be asked to review your work, and what information those experts need to make their evaluation. Understanding the audience's expectations will often allow you to anticipate expectations, questions, and even objections, so you can include the responses as part of your communication.

No matter how good your engineering work is, a communication that addresses issues other than what the audience wants will rarely be well received. A suggestion for improving computer chip design will be ignored if your listener or reader is expecting you to report on raw materials inventory.

It is often helpful to interview the targets of your communication in person or ask them by email what information they expect to get. For example, is the manager expecting you to provide recommendations for solving a problem or does he or she expect you to spell out how to implement the solution?

In addition to knowing what content the audience expects, it is also important to understand how the audience expects you to present the material. This often differs from company to company, so it might be helpful for a newly hired engineer to ask a more experienced colleague what the company standards are. There are several characteristics to be aware of:

- The kind of language used: technical vs. non-technical, informal vs. formal, restrained or enthusiastic.
- The sections of the document or presentation: many organizations have a standard form, enforced by tradition if not rule. For example, is there always an executive summary in a written report? Are supporting data generally given in a separate section or presented with recommendations?
- Length: engineers often feel that a document or presentation should be long enough to express everything they want to say. However, it is important to take into account the expectations of the audience and the organizational traditions. It is often the case that documents must be much shorter than the engineer expects.

How do audience members perceive the main issues?

Even people with similar backgrounds, desires, and organizational roles can have very different perceptions of issues. It is useful to know whether there are differences of opinion on the main issues. Not infrequently, interpersonal or organizational conflicts impact the readiness of people to accept recommendations. Some audience members might be subordinate to others; individuals and organizational units may blame one another for a recent event; one participant may have overruled another in the past. All of these emotional factors might impact receptiveness to recommendations. The more you know about them, the better prepared you will be.

The best way to find out about individuals' perceptions is to do background research. Some information can be gathered through interaction with audience members. When that is not sufficient, it may be necessary to review some background documents or speak with other people who know your audience members.

In the hospital scenario, the oral presentation is to be given to the hospital president, the Director of Nursing, the ER administrator, and several doctors and several nurses who work in the ER. The diverse audience requires a multi-faceted presentation. Include the overview and main points for the senior level people in your audience and include examples for the nurses. Encourage questions from everyone to make sure you are providing the audience with the information they expected to receive. As you present, take into account what you have learned about the interrelation of your audience members, for example, tension that has occurred at a previous time when doctors overlooked nurses' suggestions.

With regard to the written report, think about all the possible people who might read it. In the body of the report, describe all information necessary for the different readers to understand your ideas. Give credit to everyone who contributed to the study. Include all the data in appendices. If the recommendation is adopted, the changes will need to be described to lower level personnel such as the technicians who work in the ER. In an appendix, include a communication for them that describe the changes in non-technical vocabulary in a one-page document that is easy to understand.

The three tasks described above as part of analyzing your audience – finding out who is in the audience, what their expectations of the talk are, and what their perceptions of the main issues are – can take some time to complete. However, the effort is worthwhile; practicing engineers, supervisors, and senior executives have all reported that this work is necessary for communication to be effective.

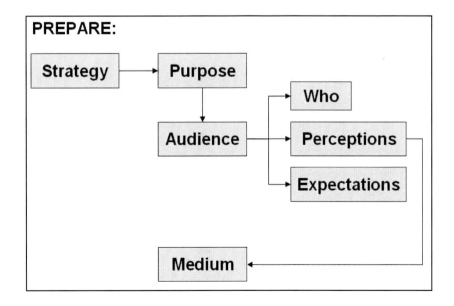

Figure 8: Medium

Medium

So far we have discussed the first two parts of preparing communication strategy: identifying the purpose of the communication and analyzing the audience. The last part of preparing strategy is choosing the right medium for your communication (Figure 8).

For oral presentations, most presenters use Microsoft PowerPoint Slides or similar visual projections. (At the time we are writing this chapter, PowerPoint has the advantage of being widely used, meaning that your slides can be sent electronically to anyone who was unable to attend the presentation.) If your slides contain many details, it might be helpful to use them as handouts so the audience can review them more easily. If audience members will need to take notes to remember specific data you discuss, hand out copies of your slides before your talk. If you plan to use any technology in your presentation, you should check to see what is available, especially if the presentation will take place in a location you are not familiar with. Make sure that the room contains the necessary projector, computer, and software – if it doesn't, you should arrange to bring your own.

With regard to written reports, you should use the word processing package that your audience is most familiar with (Microsoft Word, for example). Make the document available in electronic format and paper copies. If you work with some people who use one platform and others who use a different platform, it can be helpful to convert the document to a format that can be freely read on nearly every platform. Currently, Adobe PDF format serves this purpose well.

In the hospital scenario, standard PowerPoint slides are the safest medium for your presentation. Before the presentation is given, you should check for the availability of audiovisual equipment and bring your own if necessary. Hand out copies of the slides to make it easier for your diverse audience to follow along, take notes, and ask questions. Bring copies of your written report and CDs with electronic copies.

Now that we have finished discussing the strategy part of preparing a communication, we will describe the creation of the actual material used in your oral presentation and in your written report.

3.4.1.2 Creating the Material

In this section, we will discuss the creation of written material for communication. In some cases, like when you are producing a report, the written material will be your entire communication. In other cases, like when you are giving an oral presentation, written materials like slides and handouts will play important supporting roles in your communication.

In either case, your written materials will help direct the audience's attention, give them the information they will need for decision, and influence their motivation to implement the recommendations. The effort required to develop, evaluate, and revise these materials will pay rich dividends.

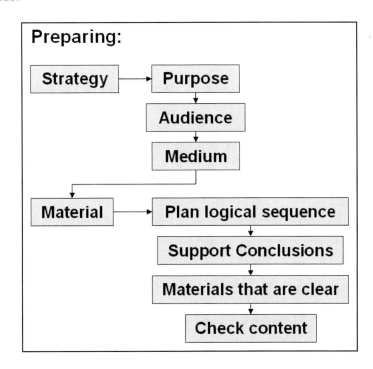

Figure 9: The Material

Creating written material for your communication involves planning the logical sequence, supporting the conclusions, making sure the ideas are clear and checking that the content is correct (Figure 9).

Planning the logical sequence

Because the purpose of engineering communication is to get people to understand new ideas and analyses, it is important that your presentation or report has a logical flow. A good example of this is your own engineering classes. When the professor gives a lecture that is logically organized so that you have all the information you need for the next step, it is much easier to understand. On the other hand, a lecture where the professor has to constantly say, "sorry, here's another equation you need to know to understand what I'm saying now" can be difficult to understand. Your engineering communications should be like the first professor's class – easy to follow and understand.

There are two important aspects to a logical flow of ideas: sequence and clustering. By **sequence**, we mean that every time you introduce a new fact or idea, you should have already given the audience enough information to understand where it fits into the bigger picture and why it is important. For example, before showing how a new chemical process will reduce benzene output by 20%, it is important to let your audience know that every percent reduction in benzene output will save your company $2 million.

The second important aspect of logical flow in engineering communication is clustering ideas. By **clustering**, we mean that you should keep ideas about the same topic together, rather than switching back and forth between topics. Compare the following two descriptions of a new manufacturing process.

The new process is an assembly line. The welding station has been moved from the beginning to the middle of the process. The new line is 62 feet long and requires only 15 workers to operate. The copper tubing adjacent to the welding station is placed in floor racks.	The new process is an assembly line. The new line is 62 feet long and requires only 15 workers to operate. The welding station has been moved from the beginning to the middle of the process. The copper tubing adjacent to the welding station is placed in floor racks.

Notice that the version on the right is easier to follow, because ideas have been clustered – the two sentences describing the line are together, as are the two sentences describing the welding station instead of switching back and forth between topics.

In putting together the sequence of ideas to use in slides for a presentation or an outline for a report, it might be helpful to think about storyboarding. The executives we interviewed emphasized this concept, which comes originally from the film industry and involves planning a series of scenes at once. To start with, the main event of each scene is set out as a way of visualizing the logical flow of the story. In the same way, the presentation or written material can be planned step by step. Write each of your main ideas on a card, and put them in order so that they are clustered and have a logical sequence. Then, add details to the cards, making sure that each detail you add fits under the card's heading.

In the hospital scenario, you should prepare both your slides and your report using this technique. To check your organization, review the titles of the slides and the headings and subheadings of your report. Are they in the right order? Make sure you have included information about the context and background before discussing the objectives of your study. For example, describe how the need for an expanded ER came about before you describe your project. Check to see that you don't get ahead of yourself with technical and medical vocabulary. For example, explain what the medical equipment in the ER is before referring to it by an abbreviated name.

Supporting Conclusions

In any communication, engineers are expected to give reasons for their recommendations. These reasons can include, for example, test results, mathematical calculations, surveys and interviews, or historical observations. The support these items provide for engineers' ideas is critical when trying to convince an unwilling or undecided audience.

Depending on the type of audience being addressed, the level of supporting detail can be very different. When presenting wind tunnel results to fellow engineers, you might describe the technical parameters of the tests; on the other hand, you might simply refer to "wind tunnel tests" when communicating with management.

Each supporting point must have a clear relationship to the idea that it is supporting. You should not assume that the connection between a supporting detail and the main idea is obvious – even if it is obvious to you. To make sure the audience sees the connection, you can repeat key words from the main idea or explicitly say why the detail supports the conclusion.

In addition to including supporting material in the slides of a presentation or the body of a written report, it can often be helpful to have extra material to be used as needed. When you give an oral presentation, there might be requests for additional detail. A strategy that many presenters find valuable is to include basic supporting material in the presentation, and have backup data on optional slides available in case of detailed questions. The same tactic can be used in a written report; the basic material can be described in the body of the report, with more detailed test results given in an appendix. The reader can then decide for himself or herself whether to read the extra material.

This approach would be useful in the hospital scenario. One of the main recommendations might be to change the procedure for moving patients from the ER to a hospital bed. A piece of supporting material might be that the results of a computer simulation predict a 25% increase in patient throughput using the new procedure. In the oral presentation, your main slide could refer to this 25% increase, and you could create an additional slide with more detail about the simulation just in case anyone in the audience is curious. The report could refer to the 25% increase in the executive summary and the body, while an appendix would include a detailed description of the simulation.

Materials that are clear

Engineers, supervisors, and senior executives all stressed the importance of creating slides and reports that are clear, easily understood, and free of distractions. If material is easy to understand, it can result in action sooner than if the material is confusing or wordy. When creating slides, the focus should be on putting down only the most important points so that the message is clear.

One of the ways that you can help make your message clear is to use **roadmapping**. Just like an interstate highway might have signs like "Dallas 20 miles" or "Elm Street next exit" to remind you of where you are (or let you know if you're lost), you can do the same thing in your oral presentations and written reports. In a written document, you can include section and subsection titles. In an oral presentation, you can alert the audience with a simple comment like "now I will describe the results of my testing."

In addition, it is helpful to remind your audience how ideas relate to each other. It can be hard for someone not as familiar as you are with the project to make the correct connections between ideas. Therefore, an effective speaker or writer clearly states (a) how each idea is related to the last one and the next one, and (b) how each idea relates to the main point. The engineering professionals we interviewed and advisors on writing agree on a general principle:

- Begin by expressing the idea
- Provide supporting detail
- Restate the idea

This sequence works for single slides or paragraphs, and for whole oral presentations or written documents. If the report is longer than a few slides or paragraphs, it is advisable to break it into sections, and develop this sequence for each section.

Engineers often need to use charts and graphs. Even though engineers are trained to quickly understand information from charts and graphs, it is often a difficult task for many readers – often more difficult than interpreting words. To help your audience understand, it is important to describe each graph, starting with the labels on each axis and continuing with each of the lines included on the graph.

In addition to keeping the materials clear and understandable, it is important to avoid distraction. When giving an oral presentation it is best to avoid most animation unless it adds to the content. For example, having a delivery truck representing the organization move across each slide looks cute, but the moving truck is likely to grab the audience's attention, distracting them from the message.

In the hospital scenario, graphics should be added to the slides for the oral presentation only when they add information. It might be helpful to show a picture of a headwall power unit (one type of ER equipment) so the audience understands what it looks like and how much space it requires. On the other hand, placing the hospital's brightly-colored logo on each slide does not add information, and could serve as a distraction if people's eyes focus on its colors. Use a non-serif font so the slides are easy to read. In the report, use headings and subheadings to guide the reader. Omit any words or phrases that do not directly relate to the purpose of the report.

Checking the content

A key component of preparing an oral presentation or written material is to check the content repeatedly for the following characteristics:

- Accuracy
- Consistency
- Impact on your audience

Check to make sure all of the information is correct and is presented in the same way throughout the presentation. Also, verify that there are no grammatical or spelling errors. Errors of this type call into question the accuracy of the information in the document – supervisors and executives say that if you don't recognize (or don't care enough to fix) these errors, they will wonder what other errors you've also made. Finally, put yourself in the place of your audience – pretend you have the same background and concerns as they do – and decide whether the audience will respond in the way you want them to.

In written and oral presentation material, it is important to plan the logical flow, provide support for conclusions, make sure the material is clear, and check the content. At this point we have covered the two main stages needed to prepare a communication: communication strategy and creating the material. Now we will turn to a topic that focuses more on oral communication: the delivery of an oral presentation.

As an expert witness, Dr. Taylor supports the conclusion that the Lap Winder was not unreasonably dangerous by raising two key points: 1) that it met OSHA standards and 2) that it had been in operation for a very long time without causing accidents. This evidence by Dr. Taylor gives further support for a jury to concur that the machine was in fact designed safely.

3.4.2 Delivery

During a presentation, the speaker has three main goals: first, staying professional; second, keeping the audience's attention; and third, conveying his or her ideas. These recommendations are all taken from interviews with engineers, supervisors, and senior executives.

3.4.2.1 Staying Professional

Projecting confidence and professionalism will show the audience how serious you are about your work, and give the impression that you are capable. On the other hand, seeming unprofessional can have the opposite effect – your audience will be less likely to believe that you are serious and capable, and will therefore be less likely to take your recommendations seriously.

The exact components to professional behavior vary from company to company, so a newly-hired engineer should learn from observation, or just ask an experienced co-worker. However, there are also several near-universal aspects of professional presentation behavior. For example, you convey a professional attitude by wearing business clothing and presenting with good posture. Answering questions clearly and honestly is another good way of showing professionalism. If you don't know an answer, say "I'm not sure, let me get back to you" – and then do just that. Answering the question correctly the next day (after doing some research) is both professional and honest, and the executives we interviewed say they depend on the answers of engineers who tell them when they are unsure of something.

3.4.2.2 Keeping the Audience's Attention

Besides staying professional as you present, you will need to work to keep the audience's attention. If the audience stops paying attention, the ideas you present will not be internalized and your recommendations will be less likely to be implemented.

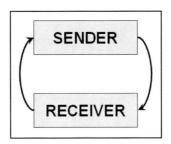

Figure 10: Two way communication

Earlier in this chapter, we discussed the organization and content of presentations. These are important tools for keeping the audience interested and attentive. In addition, there are several presentation tactics that help maintain the audience's attention. Eye contact with the audience tells them you are interested in their reactions as you present, and prevents them from looking away for too long. Answering questions is another way of keeping your listeners engaged. Be alert for hands going up in your audience. Interact with the person asking the question so you can clarify the question and make sure you answered it. A communication event always has two participants: a sender and a receiver, as shown in Figure 10. The process is two-way: the sender and the receiver swap roles. To be an effective communicator, learning to receive is as important as learning to send messages. Occasionally an important audience member will not understand one of your points, but is unwilling to ask a question. By maintaining eye contact with the audience, you might be able to recognize from that person's face that he or she is lost, and you can try to engage that person specifically.

3.4.2.3 Conveying your ideas

The main goal of any presentation is to convey your ideas. In order to get your message across, you need to use language that your audience will understand. If your audience is made up of other engineers, you will be able to use more of the technical language that you use in your engineering projects. However, if your audience includes some people who don't share your background, you will need to describe your technical ideas as you present them. For example, you might explain what "mathematical modeling" is before describing the particular model that you used.

When you use charts and graphs in your presentation, explain them to your audience. If you display a flowchart, for example, explain the parts of the chart and the relationship between those parts. Giving an example will help convey the process that you are illustrating.

In the hospital scenario, you should dress in business attire and stand up without leaning on the podium as you speak. Look at your audience as you present, and answer questions as they come up. When you show a patient flow diagram, briefly explain each step in the diagram. Since your audience includes the hospital president, the Director of Nursing, the ER administrator, and several doctors and nurses working in the ER, you can use medical terms that they will all understand. However, because they are probably unfamiliar with engineering terminology, you should be careful to define any technical terms you use.

We have completed our review of the delivery of a presentation. The key concepts we covered were staying professional, keeping your audience's attention, and conveying your ideas. Next we will describe the follow-up that is needed both after an oral presentation is given and after a written report is delivered.

3.4.3 Follow-Up

The engineers, supervisors, and senior executives we interviewed all emphasized that communication requires follow-up. The point of following up is to maintain the communication, answer questions, and make sure that your ideas are not pushed aside without reason. With regard to both oral and written communication, follow-up allows you to continue engaging the audience by asking and answering questions and by helping to resolve any disagreements. The continued interaction can also help you refine your own ideas.

In the hospital scenario, you should answer any remaining questions from your talk – anything you've had to answer "I'm not sure, let me get back to you" about. Once you've submitted the written report, get in touch with your main contacts to see what issues have come up as a result of your ideas. For example, the hospital might have decided to add new technology to the ER at the same time they expand. They might need you to tell them how that would affect your recommendations.

3.5 SUMMARY

Communication is important to having a successful career as an engineer because it is critical to getting your recommendations implemented. We described characteristics of engineering communication and how it differs from communication in everyday life.

To help you become a successful communicator, we explained how to use your knowledge of your audience and the organizational context to help determine the form and content of your communication. Then we reviewed the basics involved in preparing and delivering a communication. Preparation involves identifying the communication strategy and creating the material. Delivery includes staying professional, keeping the audience's attention, and conveying your ideas. We also noted the need to follow up with your audience afterward.

We described how these principles apply to two common types of engineering communication: oral presentations and written reports. However, the same ideas can be applied to any kind of engineering communication, ranging from the informal discussion with a fellow engineer over coffee to the formal presentation to the CEO, and ranging from informal notes taken during an impromptu discussion to formal written reports.

References

Alley, Michael, The Craft of Scientific Presentations, New York, Springer-Verlag, 2003.

Alley, Michael, The Craft of Scientific Writing, Third Edition, New York, Springer-Verlag, 1996.

Bailey, Edward P., and Powell, Philip A., The Practical Writer, Sixth Edition, Boston, Heinle, 2003.

Lannon, John M., Technical Communication, Ninth Edition, New York, Longman, 2003.

Minto, Barbara, The Pyramid Principle, Third Edition, London, Pearson Education, Limited, 2002.

Tufte, Edward R., The Visual Display of Quantitative Information, Cheshire, Conn., Graphics Press, 2001.

Williams, Joseph M., Style: Ten Lessons in Clarity and Grace. Seventh Edition, New York, Longman, 2003.

Zelazny, Gene, Say It with Charts: The Executive's Guide to Visual Communication, Fourth Edition, New York, McGraw-Hill, 2001

Zelazny, Gene, Say It with Presentations: How to Design and Deliver Successful Business Presentations, Fourth Edition, New York, McGraw-Hill, 2000

ABOUT THE AUTHORS

Judith Shaul Norback is the Director of Workplace and Academic Communication in the School of Industrial and Systems Engineering at the Georgia Institute of Technology. She can be reached at judith.norback@isye.gatech.edu.

Joel S. Sokol is an Assistant Professor of Industrial and Systems Engineering at the Georgia Institute of Technology. He can be reached at joel.sokol@isye.gatech.edu.

Peter J. McGuire is Professor and Associate Chair of the School of Literature, Communication and Culture at the Georgia Institute of Technology.

Garlie A. Forehand is a Consultant in Educational Research with the School of Industrial and Systems Engineering at the Georgia Institute of Technology.

This chapter is a product of the authors' research as part of the workplace communication initiative at the School of Industrial and Systems Engineering at the Georgia Institute of Technology, and is funded in part by the National Science Foundation under Grant DUE-0231305.

4 Engineering Ethics

LEARNING GOALS

- Explain the importance of ethics in solving engineering problems
- Define engineering ethics
- Differentiate between Utilitarianism and Kantianism
- Discuss the codes of ethics formulated by engineering societies
- Apply Utilitarianism and Kantianism in solving ethical problems
- Discuss how application of ethical concepts could lead to changes in products and procedures
- Show how ethical behavior by engineers is critical to the well-being of countries and societies

4.1 INTRODUCTION[1]

Karen White's hand trembled as she pushed open the door to her manager's office. It had been only three years since she received her engineering diploma and she felt blessed to be an engineer in P & M, the top car brake manufacturer in the country. She enjoyed her job; her co-workers were nice, she was being paid well, and the work was interesting. However, in the past three years, she had only had one personal conversation with her manager. She wondered what Mr. Jones would say when she told him that she had found a potentially fatal problem in the design of a new car brake that was being sold to a major car manufacturer. Mr. Jones let Karen into the large office and asked her to have a seat. She fidgeted as she nervously began to explain the problem. Soon, she became comfortable with her words and explained the problem and the potentially disastrous situation. When she concluded her presentation, she was surprised to hear her boss say that he knew of the problem. He continued by saying that since the brake would malfunction only in very rare circumstances, the firm would simply ignore the flaw. "You see, Karen, it is not really a very big problem and the probability of malfunction is very low. The car manufacturer has not asked us any questions. Just go on with your work. You are new, right? You wouldn't know, then, that we keep our problems to ourselves in this firm. Our customers want to hear about our success stories and our high quality standards, not our little problems. Those who make a big deal about small problems usually don't work for us." Karen left the office very shaken up yet realized that she had to make a decision. Should she risk termination and personally inform the manufacturer of the flaw or should she ignore the problem and continue with her work?

Karen has just faced an ethical dilemma. Although few want to be placed in her position, as a member of the professional engineering world, you may also be confronted with a similar situation. Many engineering companies have been sued for product failures, improper design, and copyright violations due to unethical behavior. In order to determine solutions to the various ethical issues that arise in the workplace, it is crucial for every engineer to understand what is considered to be ethical behavior in the engineering profession. The need for this ethical knowledge in professional engineering decisions has led to the development of the field of engineering ethics. This chapter introduces the Lorn Manufacturing case study as a real world connection to the concepts of engineering ethics. As definitions of engineering ethics and of ethical theories such as Kantianism and Utilitarianism are examined, the case of Jim Russell and Lorn Manufacturing will be used to illustrate ideas. In doing so, the concepts learned in this chapter can be better defined through actual events. Finally, we will learn how to use ethical theories to help quantify and solve ethical problems.

In this chapter, we define engineering ethics. Then we describe the process by which moral judgments could be arrived at. We then discuss two different ethical codes of conduct: Utilitarianism and Kantianism. We apply these codes of conduct to the scenario provided above and then conclude the chapter by describing the importance of ethics in engineering. We also connect the theories discussed in each section with examples derived from the Lorn case study.

4.2 ENGINEERING ETHICS DEFINED

Engineering ethics can be defined as (1) the activity of solving moral problems by understanding, developing, and justifying moral judgments related to engineering issues and (2) the development of and compliance to currently accepted ethical codes of conduct. It is important to understand the components of this definition before you can fully comprehend the concept of engineering ethics. Let us start by elaborating on the individual terms, moral judgments and ethics, in the first part of the definition.

4.2.1: Moral Judgments

Ethics is the study of morals and moral judgements.[2] *What are moral judgments?* The words **moral** and **ethical** have similar meanings:

Right	=	Moral	=	Ethical
Wrong	=	Immoral	=	Unethical

Here are few examples that illustrate these similarities:

(1) The right (ethical, moral) thing to do is to return stolen money.
(2) It is wrong (immorally, unethically) to rob a bank.[3]

These two examples are **normative statements**. Normative ethical statements take a judgmental attitude toward morals in order to guide actions. In the first example, a judgment is being made upon the action of returning stolen money in order to convince the listener to return the money. **Descriptive ethical statements** are those statements that take a neutral attitude toward morals. For example, a descriptive ethical statement may be "She bribed the official." The normative ethical statement would be "It was wrong for her to bribe the official."

Aside from moral and immoral, two other concepts are **amoral** and **nonmoral**. Amorality describes those people who truly do not know right from wrong. A small child or a mental psychopath could be classified as amoral. Nonmoral is not a moral statement. Nonmoral not equal to immoral.

Consider these two examples of nonmoral statements:

(1) It is right (correct) to say the earth is round.
(2) It is wrong (incorrect) to say the earth is flat.

Although these statements use the words "right" and "wrong," they are not ethical or moral judgments since they do not deal with a person, but an abstract entity, "earth." But, consider the following sentence:

Socrates lived during the time of the transition from the height of the Athenian Empire to its decline after its defeat by Sparta and its allies in the Peloponnesian War. At a time when Athens was seeking to recover from humiliating defeat, the Athenian public court was induced by three leading public figures to try Socrates for impiety and for corrupting the youth of Athens. According to Dr. Will Beldam, Socrates was the first person to question everything and everyone, and apparently it offended the leaders of this time. He was found guilty as charged, and sentenced to drink hemlock, which cost him his life[4].

When considering this statement, your judgment might be that the decision by the courts at that time was either right or wrong. Then you are making a moral statement as the resulting decision impacts the life of a human being. Moral judgments deal with implications of using technology in a social situation rather than the scientific fact or discovery itself.

4.2.2: Ethics Defined

The following quotes are definitions of ethics from various authors:

Webster's Dictionary:
> Main Entry: eth-ic
> Pronunciation: 'e-thik
> Function: noun
> 1 plural but singular or plural in construction: the discipline dealing with what is good and bad and with moral duty and obligation
> 2 a: a set of moral principles or values
>   b: a theory or system of moral values
>   <the present-day materialistic ethic>
>   c: the principles of conduct governing an individual or a group
>   <professional ethics>
>   d: a guiding philosophy[5]

J.T. Stevenson:

> Ethics is concerned with standards for right conduct, with justice and injustice, with virtue and vice, with our duties and rights in a community. It is also concerned with what is good or valuable, what is worth pursuing, what is prudent, rational conduct...[6]

Carolyn Csongradi:

> Ethics is a discipline, which attempts to examine and understand ways in which choices are made involving issues of right and wrong.[7]

Case Western Reserve University Business Ethics:

> The term "ethics" is used in several different ways. First, it means the study of morals. It is also the name for that branch of philosophy concerned with the nature of morals and moral evaluation e.g., what is right and wrong, virtuous or vicious, and beneficial or harmful (to others).[8]

Let us clarify these definitions by saying that ethics is concerned with assessing what is right and wrong, good and bad, or just and unjust in situations. *Now that we have explained what ethics means, we can better answer the question "What are moral judgements?" Moral judgements are those judgements concerned with standards of right conduct, justice and injustice, virtue and vice, and our duties and rights in a community.*

4.3 UNDERSTANDING, DEVELOPING, AND JUSTIFYING MORAL JUDGEMENTS

Look again at the first part of the engineering ethics definition: "Engineering ethics is the activity of solving moral problems by understanding, developing, and justifying moral judgements related to engineering issues."

Now, we may ask the question: *How does one solve moral problems?* In order to assess any ethical problem and develop a moral judgment, you must determine which actions are moral and which are immoral. How can anyone decide if an action is moral or immoral? To answer this question, philosophers have developed many different approaches to values to help judge the moral significance of any deed. Two of these approaches, Utilitarianism and Kantianism, can be very useful in understanding and developing moral judgments.

4.3.1: Ethical Universalism/Utilitarianism

Utilitarianism, championed by John Stuart Mill and Jeremy Bentham, is founded upon the **principle of utility**, which states that the goal of every action is to provide the greatest balance of good (happiness) over bad (unhappiness). It seems evident that this principle is at the core of all actions. Whether choosing clothes, ice cream, employees, colleges, or spouses, people try to choose the option that will create the happiest situation.

Mill and Bentham expanded upon the idea of utility by stating that ethical actions are those moral actions that create the greatest amount of happiness. This is very different than many other ethical ideas because its guiding principle is equality. **Bentham's dictum** states that each person must be counted equally and every person can only count as one unit. Each person is a singular container of satisfaction and *every* person must be taken into consideration when making an ethical decision. Utilitarianism focuses on the consequences that occur from the actions. Using these ideas, Utilitarianism becomes a quantifiable method of proving ethical behavior.

Suppose that there is a room with twenty people, and eighteen people feel that the consequences of murder will bring them unhappiness and two people feel that the consequences of murder will bring them happiness. Each person is a singular container of satisfaction, but every person must be considered together to make the ethical decision. There would be a greater balance of happiness over unhappiness when murder does not take place, and murder would be considered an unethical action in that group.

Mill bases many of his societal theories upon Bentham's dictum. He argues that a wretched worldwide social structure is the reason for unhappiness in the world. Mill believes that the lack of equality due to fame, wealth, and power, creates an unhappy populace. For example, a person may consider a Congressman's opinion to be a hundred times as important as an average college student's opinion. According to Mill, if every college student was treated with as much importance as every Congressman, then there would be a much more pleasant social system.

The principles of Utilitarianism can be applied to engineering situations where ethical problems arise. Imagine that you have just engineered a multi-million dollar product that would bring large profits to a manufacturing company and a large bonus to you. Unfortunately, the product emits many toxic gases that could severely harm the citizens of a town. Suppose that fifty people own the company and there are a thousand people in the town. You consider the opinion of one of these fifty people to equal 500 citizens' opinions since you realize that pleasing those 50 people could help you place a down payment on a new house. The citizens will provide you with no direct benefits. However, using Bentham's dictum, each person must be considered equal regardless of what benefits and interrelations you have with him/her. Fifty-one people would receive happiness from this product and 1000 people would receive unhappiness from the product. Therefore, according to Bentham's dictum, although you might want the company to market the product, to actually produce the product would be an immoral action since unhappiness outweighs happiness.

The major problem with the Utilitarianism view is that it is practically impossible to quantify a large group's feelings about an event. In most situations, a few people make decisions for a vast number of people. It would be impossible to ask every person's perceptions about every issue. Therefore, decision-makers guess what other people feel and make decisions in a democratic fashion. Due to this difficulty in measuring feelings, many argue that Utilitarianism is not the best method for judging the morality of an action.

4.3.2: Kantianism

Immanuel Kant, an 18th century Enlightenment thinker, provides a strikingly different approach to determining ethical behavior. While Utilitarians base their ideas upon the view of humans as containers of satisfaction, Kant views a human as an **autonomous being**. A human is autonomous if he/she: (1) has the ability to make rational decisions, (2) has the ability to act responsibly, (3) is an **agent** responsible for an action. An agent is a person that performs an action with full knowledge of a situation, full reasoning ability, the ability to perform the actions involved in the situation, and the ability to act freely.

A person would **not** be an agent in the following situations:

(1) A man signs a contract with thieves without knowing that the men are thieves.
(2) An infant drops a gun and shoots a man.
(3) A man is accused of drowning another man in the middle of a river even though the accused man cannot swim.
(4) A man robs a bank because others are pointing a gun at him.

For Kant, this human autonomy is extremely valuable, and human autonomy becomes the basis of his **categorical imperative**. The categorical imperative states that a person should **always** treat **every** person as an autonomous being. In other words, Kant argues that the goal of ethics should not be to maximize satisfactions but to allow every person to act as an autonomous agent. Therefore, if you are an autonomous being and you should treat everyone as an autonomous being, you should treat everyone, as you would want to be treated. Kant's philosophy can be simplified to an elegant version of the rules, "Do to others what you would have them do to you" or "Act only on the rules that you wish to become universal rules."

Look again at the engineering issues discussed in the ethical Universalism / Utilitarianism section. In that section, we decided that it would be unethical to manufacture the multi-million dollar product because there would be consequences that created a greater amount of dissatisfaction than satisfaction. How can we decide if the manufacturing of the product is ethical using Kantianism? As the engineer you must consider every person as an autonomous agent. If the citizens did not have full knowledge about the product, then the citizens are not autonomous agents. You would be using them as a means to reach your own ends. Kant's categorical imperative argues that you must not ever use any other person as a means to reach your own ends. Therefore, using Kantianism, we must decide that manufacturing the product would be an unethical action. If all the people in the town were aware of the consequences and agreed to manufacture the product in order to obtain jobs, then according to Kantianism, manufacturing the product would be an ethical action.

4.3.3: Solving Moral Problems

Knowing all this, we may now answer our initial question: How can one solve moral problems? Moral problems are solved by developing moral judgments upon an action **and** choosing the best action.

We know how to develop moral judgements about situations using both Utilitarianism and Kantianism. Using Utilitarianism, the most ethical action would be the action that creates the greatest amount of satisfaction over dissatisfaction. Using Kantianism, the most ethical action would be the action that treats all people as autonomous agents. To solve a moral problem, one must decide which is the most ethical action using approaches such as these.

For many people, guidance on solving moral problems comes from a more personal source: their religion. Each religion; be it Christian, Islam, Judaism, or some other faith; teaches its followers moral guidelines that can be used to help solve moral problems. It should be noted that both Kantianism and Utilitarianism can be used in conjunction with most religious principles. After all, the main ideas behind both theories have similarities with ideas found in religious texts. When dealing with moral problems, having multiple sources from which to analyze potential solutions can be quite beneficial.

The process of understanding, developing, and justifying moral judgements can be tedious, especially when a large number of people are involved. For this reason, many organizations have developed ethical codes of conduct that guide people to act ethically in their professions. These ethical codes are based upon the philosophical approaches such as the ones that we have just studied. We will now look at the development of these ethical codes of conduct and their usefulness as we examine the second part of the definition of engineering ethics.

4.4 ETHICAL CODES OF CONDUCT

Let us look at the definition of engineering ethics: "Engineering ethics is the development of and compliance to currently accepted engineering ethical codes of conduct." Ethical codes of conduct, or **moral codes**, are simply compilations of ethical actions that act as guides to our lives. For example, the individual ethical actions "Help your neighbor," "Do not kill people," and "Do not steal" may be collected in one moral code to help guide a person to live an ethical life. Each individual ethical action in a moral code could be justified using the Utilitarian or Kantian approach. Moral codes describe the ethical actions that we should be able to find through our intuitive use of these approaches.

Engineering codes of ethics are based upon general codes of ethics. The engineering codes of ethics are simply compilations of ethical actions that act as a guide to professional life. Every moral rule in these codes could be justified using the Utilitarian or Kantian approach. Every engineering code of ethics leaves room for an engineer to make virtuous choices within his profession while instructing the engineer in the most ethical actions and procedures.

It is critical that all engineers comply with the various accepted codes. Although most of the different engineering codes have similar ideals, nearly every major engineering association has its own code. In this chapter, we shall look mainly at the National Society of Professional Engineers (NSPE) Code of Ethics (Appendix 1).

4.5 APPLYING CODES OF ENGINEERING ETHICS TO PROBLEM

Now that we have introduced the concepts of moral judgements and codes of ethics, let us now apply them to Karen's ethical problem first discussed at the beginning of the chapter:

Karen White's hand trembled as she pushed open the door to her manager's office. It had been only three years since she received her engineering diploma and she felt blessed to be an engineer in P & M, the top car brake manufacturer in the country. She enjoyed her job: her co-workers were nice, she was being paid well, and the work was interesting. However, in the past three years she had only had one personal confrontation with her manager. She wondered what Mr. Jones would say when she told him that she had found a potentially fatal problem in the design of a new car brake that was being sold to a major car manufacturer. Mr. Jones let Karen into the large office and asked her to have a seat. She fidgeted as she nervously began to explain the problem. Soon, she became comfortable with her words and explained the problem and the potentially disastrous situation. When she concluded her presentation, she was surprised to hear her boss say that he knew of the problem. He continued by saying that since the brake would malfunction only in very rare circumstances, the firm would simply ignore the flaw. "You see, Karen, it is not really a very big problem and the probability of malfunction is very low. The car manufacturer has not asked us any questions. Just go on with your work. You are new, right? You wouldn't know, then, that we keep our problems to ourselves in this firm. Our customers want to hear about our success stories and our high quality standards, not our little problems. Those who make a big deal about small problems usually don't work for us." Karen left the office very shaken up yet realized that she had to make a decision. Should she risk termination and personally inform the car manufacturer of the flaw or should she ignore the problem and continue with her work?

We can apply the NSPE code of ethics, Utilitarianism, and Kantianism to solve this moral dilemma.

4.5.1: Application of NSPE Code of Ethics

Karen could solve this problem by just applying the NSPE Code of Ethics to her situation. If Karen did **not** inform the car manufacturer of the brake flaw, she would be violating the following ethical guidelines:

NSPE II.1:   Hold paramount the safety, health, and welfare of the public.

NSPE II.1.a: If engineers' judgment is overruled under circumstances that endanger life or property, they shall notify their employer or client and such other authority as may be appropriate.

NSPE II.4:   Engineers shall act for each employer or client as faithful agents or trustees.

Since Karen would be violating a large number of ethical guidelines by not informing the manufacturer, the ethical action must be to inform the manufacturer of the flaw. Therefore, by applying the code of ethics to her situation, Karen should decide to inform the manufacturer of the flaw since it is the most ethical action.

4.5.2: Application of Utilitarianism

Let us try to solve the "Karen White" problem by applying the concepts of Utilitarianism. With Utilitarianism, every person must be considered equally and under no circumstances can any person be treated more importantly than any other person. This includes Karen, herself. Karen cannot consider her problems to be more important than the problems of a stranger. Since Utilitarianism tries to quantify moral issues, we will look at several scenarios of the same situation.

Scenario 1

Let us assume that 100 people work for the engineering firm and 800 people work for the car manufacturer. <u>One million cars are sold and it is estimated that the brake will fail in 1 out of every 10,000 cars.</u>

Let us now weigh the different options to decide which option will create a greater balance of happiness over unhappiness. Positive numbers will show happiness and negative numbers will show unhappiness.

(1) Ignore the Problem and Continue Working:

Benefit / Not Beneficial	Amount of People
+ Benefits Karen since she will not lose her job	+ 1
+ Benefits the others in P&M (Can't include Karen again)	+ 99
+ Benefits the car manufacturer because they have delays	+ 800
- Will not benefit the people who have failed cars. (1/10,000 * 1 million)	– 100
Total	**800**

(2) Inform Manufacturer About Problem

Benefit / Not Beneficial	Amount of People
– Will not benefit Karen since she may lose her job	– 1
– May not benefit employees of W&M	– 99
– May not benefit car manufacturer	– 800
+ Will benefit people who won't have failed cars	+ 100
Total	**– 800**

From these figures we can conclude that the ethical action would be not to inform the manufacturer about the problems since 800 more people would become unhappy.

Scenario 2

In the second scenario, let us assume that the only change is that <u>engineers now estimate that 1 out of every 1,000 cars have their brakes fail because of the faulty design</u>. In this case, we have the following figures:

(1) Ignore the Problem and Continue Working:

Benefit / Not Beneficial	Amount of People
– Benefits Karen since she will not lose her job	+ 1
– Benefits the others in P&M	+ 99
– Benefits the car manufacturer because they won't	+ 800

have delays
– Will not benefit the people who have failed cars.   – 1000
 (-1/1000 * 1 million)

Total   – 100

(2) Inform Manufacturer About Problem

Benefit / Not Beneficial	**Amount of People**
– Will not benefit Karen since she may lose her job	– 1
– May not benefit employees of W&M	– 99
– May not benefit car manufacturer	– 800
+ Will benefit people who won't have failed cars	+ 1000

Total   + 100

The ethical action in this scenario would be to inform the manufacturer since 100 more people would benefit from that action.

Scenario 3

In the third scenario, let us assume that the only change is that engineers now estimate that 1 out of every 1,000,000 cars have their brakes fail because of the faulty design. In this case, we have the following figures:

(1) Ignore the Problem and Continue Working:

Benefit / Not Beneficial	**Amount of People**
– Benefits Karen since she will not lose her job	+ 1
– Benefits the others in P&M	+ 99
– Benefits the car manufacturer because they won't have delays	+ 800
– Will not benefit the people who have failed cars. (-1/1 million * 1 million)	– 1

Total   899

(2) Inform Manufacturer About Problem

Benefit / Not Beneficial	**Amount of People**
– Will not benefit Karen since she may lose her job	– 1
– May not benefit employees of W&M	– 99
– May not benefit car manufacturer	– 800
+ Will benefit people who won't have failed cars	+ 1

An ethical action in this scenario would be not to inform the manufacturer since 899 more people would benefit. Karen has to agree with her manager that this is a minor problem that need not be reported to the manufacturer and public.

Comparison

Each of these three scenarios offers different solutions. Scenario 2 suggests that Karen should inform the manufacturer of the flaw while Scenarios 1 and 3 recommends that Karen not inform the manufacturer. Unlike the ethical codes that gave one clear answer for every scenario, Utilitarianism offers different answers depending upon the scenario. If we use Utilitarianism without knowledge of the probabilities, it is unclear if Karen should inform the manufacturer of the flaw. Estimating the probabilities becomes the major issue in using this theory. Karen as an engineer has to answer the question: how serious is the design flaw in the new car brake? At the end, she has to make an ethical decision on whether to inform the car manufacturer, tell the public, or keep quiet.

4.5.3: Application of Kantianism

If we apply Kantianism to Karen White's situation, we must focus on individual autonomy and not the final consequences of her actions. If Karen does not inform the manufacturer of her knowledge of the flaw, the manufacturer would not have full knowledge of the situation when installing the brakes into their cars. In other words, the manufacturer would not be a fully autonomous agent. Since Kantianism argues that everyone in a situation must be a fully autonomous agent for the action to be ethical, this would not be an ethical action. Unlike Utilitarianism, Kantianism gives one definite answer and does not allow room for exceptions in different scenarios. If Karen informs the car manufacturer against her boss's advice, the car manufacturer might choose to ignore Karen's recommendation. Then Karen has to deal with the ethical dilemma: should I make a public statement? Even then, the public might ignore her warning. If she has informed all potential users and they ignore her warning, then Karen has performed ethically using Kantianism.

4.6 DISCREPANCIES IN ETHICAL ANALYSIS

As we have seen in Karen White's case, different ethical approaches result in different solutions. Usually, it is best and simplest to follow the rules given in codes of ethics. However, in many instances, codes of ethics may not give enough information to fully analyze a situation. In these scenarios, it is wise to use Utilitarianism or Kantianism to achieve a solution.

In Karen's case, our Kantian and Utilitarian analyses resulted in different solutions due to the different scenarios. This illustrates the difficulty in determining truly moral actions since there often is not a definite line that says that one thing is "wrong" or "right." To complicate matters more, ethical values vary across national boundaries and cultures. For example, some countries do not consider copyright as an individual right whereas other countries guarantee the right to an individual / organization. In some countries, legal documents define the contract, and engineers are often advised to "put all design details in writing" in order to protect one's interest. In other countries, verbal agreements carry a significantly greater weight than legal documents, so engineering design details are not documented extensively. These disparities may allow a company to ethically adopt different manufacturing standards throughout the world.

In this section, we have established a guideline for solving moral problems. However, the manager or engineer must make the final decision based upon the circumstances surrounding an individual event.

4.7 THE IMPORTANCE OF ETHICS IN ENGINEERING

The example in the earlier section shows that making an ethical engineering decision is difficult. It will become more difficult as engineering and sciences change the modes of life drastically in the future. The value judgments made in the work force not only impact the profitability and reputation of your company but also directly affects your reputation and character.

Faching (1993) dramatically illustrates the importance of good ethical judgement in all engineering situations with his dark warning of a heartless bureaucratic civilization:

> Our modern technological civilization offers us seemingly infinite utopian opportunities to recreate ourselves (e.g., genetic engineering, behavioral engineering) and our societies (social engineering) and our world (chemical engineering, atomic

engineering). But having transcended all limits and all norms, we seem bereft of a normative vision to govern the use of our utopian techniques. This normlessness threatens us with demonic self-destruction. It is this dark side of technical civilization that was revealed to us not only at Auschwitz but also at Hiroshima.

The heart of a bureaucratic social order is the secularization of professional roles within the bureaucratic structure such that technical experts completely identify themselves with their roles as experts in the use of techniques while totally surrendering the question of what those technical skills will be used for to the expertise of those above them in the bureaucratic hierarchy.

Thus whereas technological production gives persons a sense of creativity and potency and even self-transcendence as one overcomes obstacles and realizes a goal, bureaucracy creates just the opposite; namely, a sense of impotency, helplessness, and the necessity to conform to a reality so real, massive, and all pervasive that "nothing can be changed." The result is a social structure that separates ends from means and deciders from actors, relegating all decisions to "higher levels." Such a social structure prepares the way for the demonic, preventing ethical questions from ever arising even as it creates bureaucratic individuals who feel no personal responsibility for their actions.

The presence of theonomous (i.e., self-transcending) holy communities (both religious and secular), including technical and professional societies, who surrender to the genuine questions of their discipline and resist the monolithic incursion of the techno-bureaucratic political myths, is absolutely essential to the sustaining the dignity of human life.

In the work force, you will be faced with ethical decisions that may change many lives. Taking responsibility for one's own actions is the key to making true moral decisions. If all professionals take this responsibility to act ethically in the work place, engineering and technology will not only sustain but could enhance the dignity of human life.

4.8 SUMMARY

This chapter defines engineering ethics and explores some ways that engineers can solve moral issues, using Utilitarianism, Kantianism, and codes of ethics. The appendix contains an example of a code of ethics that should be studied to understand what a professional society expects of its members. The appendix also provides references to code of ethics for different fields in engineering. These codes should be helpful to you as you make decisions in your job. The results of the decisions will impact you, your division, company, and the public. This chapter also includes opinions about ethics and its importance in the engineering profession. As future engineers in a changing world, it is critical that you understand the necessity for ethical actions in the work place, and have the ability to extrapolate how ethical decisions can affect others.

SHORT ESSAY QUESTIONS

1) Define ethics.
2) Define engineering ethics.
3) What are moral judgements?
4) What are the fundamentals of Utilitarianism?
5) What are the fundamentals of Kantianism?
6) What is a moral code?
7) Give a few examples of engineering codes of ethics.
8) Give the fundamental canons of the NSPE Code of Ethics.
9) Can you defend the theory that every person should be treated equally? For example, should one living happy person be equal to the death of one person? Or should the death of a person be equal to the happiness of 20 people?

STUDENT ASSIGNMENT

You are in charge of an independent lab that tests residential manufactured fireplaces. The standards prescribed by the Underwriters Laboratories (UL) required the tester to place different brands into the fireplace and monitor the temperature. The fire has to be held for about 30 minutes and the fireplace could not exceed the set temperature for it pass. These temperature tests were done to assure UL that a fire could be lit inside a house and the house would not catch on fire. These tests are more demanding than the typical homeowner's usage of the manufactured fireplace in order to assure a high factor of safety. It is possible to make a fireplace pass the test by Underwriters Laboratories by adapting a few "tricks." These tricks were:

a) Move the brand toward the front of the fireplace, a little bit, thereby reducing the temperatures.
b) Place the brand very gently and do not drop it. Then the fire burns a lot longer and the heat gets released over a longer period of time.

Analyze the manufactured fireplace case study using Utilitarianism. Your two options are:

1) A fireplace passes by tweaking the tests. The fireplace would not have passed if a complete stranger had run it through the test.
2) A fireplace passes without tweaking the tests. The fireplace would have passed if a complete stranger had run it through the test.

Remember that there is a high margin of safety built into the tests. Use different figures to achieve your answer.

1. Analyze the manufacturing fireplace case study using Kantianism. Use the same two options in Problem 5.
2. Analyze the manufacturing fireplace case study using codes of ethics. Use the same two options in Problem 5.
3. Using your analysis in Problem 5, Problem 7, and Problem 11 make a decision about the system used to test manufacturing fireplaces. Are the standards good standards or should they be more precise? Is there such a thing as too much precision? Or should the engineers take it upon themselves not to take advantage of the imprecision of the standards?

GLOSSARY

Amoral: not knowing right from wrong (ethical from unethical)

Bentham's dictum: each person must be counted equally and every person can only count as one unit

Categorical Imperative: Immanuel Kant's theory that you must treat every person as an autonomous being; this is the foundation for his ethical doctrine

Descriptive statements: these statements that take a neutral attitude toward morals

Engineering ethics: (1) the activity of understanding, resolving, and justifying moral judgments related to engineering issues and (2) the development of and compliance to currently accepted ethical codes of conduct

Ethical: right, moral in certain situations

Ethics: the study of morals and moral judgments

Immoral: wrong, unethical in certain situations

Kantianism: ethical doctrine that is founded on the categorical imperative

Moral: right, ethical in certain situations

Moral Codes: compilations of ethical actions that act as guides to our lives

Nonethical: not moral judgments and have a right or wrong answer

Nonmoral: not ethical judgments and have a right or wrong answer

Normative ethics/statements: take a judgmental attitude toward morals in order to guide actions

Principle of utility: goal of every action is the greatest balance of happiness over unhappiness

Right: moral and ethical in certain situations; correct in nonmoral situations

Unethical: wrong, immoral in certain situations

Utilitarianism: ethical doctrine founded upon principle of utility

Whistleblowing: a person in a lower position who attempts to stop a higher authority's immoral actions

Wrong: immoral, unethical in certain situations; incorrect in nonmoral situations

APPENDIX 1: PROFESSIONAL ENGINEERING CODES OF ETHICS

Appendix 1: NSPE Code of Ethics for Engineers[9]

Preamble

Engineering is an important and learned profession. As members of this profession, engineers are expected to exhibit the highest standards of honesty and integrity. Engineering has a direct and vital impact on the quality of life for all people. Accordingly, the services provided by engineers require honesty, impartiality, fairness and equity, and must be dedicated to the protection of the public health, safety, and welfare. Engineers must perform under a standard of professional behavior that requires adherence to the highest principles of ethical conduct.

I. Fundamental Canons

Engineers, in the fulfillment of their professional duties, shall:

1. Hold paramount the safety, health and welfare of the public.
2. Perform services only in areas of their competence.
3. Issue public statements only in an objective and truthful manner.
4. Act for each employer or client as faithful agents or trustees.
5. Avoid deceptive acts.
6. Conduct themselves honorably, responsibly, ethically, and lawfully so as to enhance the honor, reputation, and usefulness of the profession.

II. Rules of Practice

1. Engineers shall hold paramount the safety, health, and welfare of the public.

   a. If engineers' judgment is overruled under circumstances that endanger life or property, they shall notify their employer or client and such other authority as may be appropriate.
   b. Engineers shall approve only those engineering documents that are in conformity with applicable standards.
   c. Engineers shall not reveal facts, data or information without the prior consent of the client or employer except as authorized or required by law or this Code.
   d. Engineers shall not permit the use of their name or associate in business ventures with any person or firm that they believe is engaged in fraudulent or dishonest enterprise.

e. Engineers having knowledge of any alleged violation of this Code shall report thereon to appropriate professional bodies and, when relevant, also to public authorities, and cooperate with the proper authorities in furnishing such information or assistance as may be required.

2. Engineers shall perform services only in the areas of their competence.

   a. Engineers shall undertake assignments only when qualified by education or experience in the specific technical fields involved.
   b. Engineers shall not affix their signatures to any plans or documents dealing with subject matter in which they lack competence, nor to any plan or document not prepared under their direction and control.
   c. Engineers may accept assignments and assume responsibility for coordination of an entire project and sign and seal the engineering documents for the entire project, provided that each technical segment is signed and sealed only by the qualified engineers who prepared the segment.

3. Engineers shall issue public statements only in an objective and truthful manner.

   a. Engineers shall be objective and truthful in professional reports, statements, or testimony. They shall include all relevant and pertinent information in such reports, statements, or testimony, which should bear the date indicating when it was current.
   b. Engineers may express publicly technical opinions that are founded upon knowledge of the facts and competence in the subject matter.
   c. Engineers shall issue no statements, criticisms, or arguments on technical matters that are inspired or paid for by interested parties, unless they have prefaced their comments by explicitly identifying the interested parties on whose behalf they are speaking and by revealing the existence of any interest the engineers may have in the matters.

4. Engineers shall act for each employer or client as faithful agents or trustees.

   a. Engineers shall disclose all known or potential conflicts of interest that could influence or appear to influence their judgment or the quality of their services.
   b. Engineers shall not accept compensation, financial or otherwise, from more than one party for services on the same project, or for services pertaining to the same project, unless the circumstances are fully disclosed and agreed to by all interested parties.
   c. Engineers shall not solicit or accept financial or other valuable

consideration, directly or indirectly, from outside agents in connection with the work for which they are responsible.

    d. Engineers in public service as members, advisors, or employees of a governmental or quasi-governmental body or department shall not participate in decisions with respect to services solicited or provided by them or their organizations in private or public engineering practice.

    e. Engineers shall not solicit or accept a contract from a governmental body on which a principal or officer of their organization serves as a member.

5. Engineers shall avoid deceptive acts.

    a. Engineers shall not falsify their qualifications or permit misrepresentation of their or their associates' qualifications. They shall not misrepresent or exaggerate their responsibility in or for the subject matter of prior assignments. Brochures or other presentations incident to the solicitation of employment shall not misrepresent pertinent facts concerning employers, employees, associates, joint venturers, or past accomplishments.

    b. Engineers shall not offer, give, solicit or receive, either directly or indirectly, any contribution to influence the award of a contract by public authority, or which may be reasonably construed by the public as having the effect of intent to influencing the awarding of a contract. They shall not offer any gift or other valuable consideration in order to secure work. They shall not pay a commission, percentage, or brokerage fee in order to secure work, except to a bona fide employee or bona fide established commercial or marketing agencies retained by them.

III. Professional Obligations

1. Engineers shall be guided in all their relations by the highest standards of honesty and integrity.

    a. Engineers shall acknowledge their errors and shall not distort or alter the facts.

    b. Engineers shall advise their clients or employers when they believe a project will not be successful.

    c. Engineers shall not accept outside employment to the detriment of their regular work or interest. Before accepting any outside engineering employment they will notify their employers.

    d. Engineers shall not attempt to attract an engineer from another employer by false or misleading pretenses.

    e. Engineers shall not actively participate in strikes, picket lines, or other collective coercive action.

f. Engineers shall not promote their own interest at the expense of the dignity and integrity of the profession.

2. Engineers shall at all times strive to serve the public interest.

    a. Engineers shall seek opportunities to participate in civic affairs; career guidance for youths; and work for the advancement of the safety, health and well-being of their community.
    b. Engineers shall not complete, sign, or seal plans and/or specifications that are not in conformity with applicable engineering standards. If the client or employer insists on such unprofessional conduct, they shall notify the proper authorities and withdraw from further service on the project.
    c. Engineers shall endeavor to extend public knowledge and appreciation of engineering and its achievements.

3. Engineers shall avoid all conduct or practice that deceives the public.

    a. Engineers shall avoid the use of statements containing a material misrepresentation of fact or omitting a material fact.
    b. Consistent with the foregoing, Engineers may advertise for recruitment of personnel.
    c. Consistent with the foregoing, Engineers may prepare articles for the lay or technical press, but such articles shall not imply credit to the author for work performed by others.

4. Engineers shall not disclose, without consent, confidential information concerning the business affairs or technical processes of any present or former client or employer, or public body on which they serve.

    a. Engineers shall not, without the consent of all interested parties, promote or arrange for new employment or practice in connection with a specific project for which the Engineer has gained particular and specialized knowledge.
    b. Engineers shall not, without the consent of all interested parties, participate in or represent an adversary interest in connection with a specific project or proceeding in which the Engineer has gained particular specialized knowledge on behalf of a former client or employer.

5. Engineers shall not be influenced in their professional duties by conflicting interests.

    a. Engineers shall not accept financial or other considerations, including free engineering designs, from material or equipment suppliers for specifying their product.

b. Engineers shall not accept commissions or allowances, directly or indirectly, from contractors or other parties dealing with clients or employers of the Engineer in connection with work for which the Engineer is responsible.

6. Engineers shall not attempt to obtain employment or advancement or professional engagements by untruthfully criticizing other engineers, or by other improper or questionable methods.

a. Engineers shall not request, propose, or accept a commission on a contingent basis under circumstances in which their judgment may be compromised.
b. Engineers in salaried positions shall accept part-time engineering work only to the extent consistent with policies of the employer and in accordance with ethical considerations.
c. Engineers shall not, without consent, use equipment, supplies, laboratory, or office facilities of an employer to carry on outside private practice.

7. Engineers shall not attempt to injure, maliciously or falsely, directly or indirectly, the professional reputation, prospects, practice, or employment of other engineers. Engineers who believe others are guilty of unethical or illegal practice shall present such information to the proper authority for action.

a. Engineers in private practice shall not review the work of another engineer for the same client, except with the knowledge of such engineer, or unless the connection of such engineer with the work has been terminated.
b. Engineers in governmental, industrial, or educational employ are entitled to review and evaluate the work of other engineers when so required by their employment duties.
c. Engineers in sales or industrial employ are entitled to make engineering comparisons of represented products with products of other suppliers.

8. Engineers shall accept personal responsibility for their professional activities, provided, however, that Engineers may seek indemnification for services arising out of their practice for other than gross negligence, where the Engineer's interests cannot otherwise be protected.

a. Engineers shall conform to state registration laws in the practice of engineering.
b. Engineers shall not use association with a nonengineer, a corporation, or partnership as a "cloak" for unethical acts.

9. Engineers shall give credit for engineering work to those to whom credit is due, and will recognize the proprietary interests of others.

    a. Engineers shall, whenever possible, name the person or persons who may be individually responsible for designs, inventions, writings, or other accomplishments.

    b. Engineers using designs supplied by a client recognize that the designs remain the property of the client and may not be duplicated by the Engineer for others without express permission.

    c. Engineers, before undertaking work for others in connection with which the Engineer may make improvements, plans, designs, inventions, or other records that may justify copyrights or patents, should enter into a positive agreement regarding ownership.

    d. Engineers' designs, data, records, and notes referring exclusively to an employer's work are the employer's property. Employer should indemnify the Engineer for use of the information for any purpose other than the original purpose.

As Revised July 1996

APPENDIX 2: AMERICAN SOCIETY OF MECHANICAL ENGINEERS (ASME) CODE OF ETHICS[10]

ETHICS

ASME requires ethical practice by each of its members and has adopted the following Code of Ethics of Engineers as referenced in the ASME Constitution, Article C2.1.1.

CODE OF ETHICS OF ENGINEERS

The Fundamental Principles

Engineers uphold and advance the integrity, honor and dignity of the engineering profession by:

  I. Using their knowledge and skill for the enhancement of human welfare;
 II. Being honest and impartial, and serving with fidelity the public, their employers and clients; and
III. Striving to increase the competence and prestige of the engineering profession.

The Fundamental Canons

1. Engineers shall hold paramount the safety, health, and welfare of the public in the performance of their professional duties.
2. Engineers shall perform services only in the areas of their competence.
3. Engineers shall continue their professional development throughout their careers and shall provide opportunities for the professional and ethical development of those engineers under their supervision.
4. Engineers shall act in professional matters for each employer or client as faithful agents or trustees, and shall avoid conflicts of interest or the appearance of conflicts of interest.
5. Engineers shall build their professional reputation on the merit of their services and shall not compete unfairly with others.
6. Engineers shall issue public statements only in an objective and truthful manner.

THE ASME CRITERIA
FOR INTERPRETATION OF THE CANONS

The ASME criteria for interpretation of the Canons are guidelines and represent the objectives toward which members of the engineering profession should strive. They are principles, which an engineer can reference, in specific situations. In addition, they provide interpretive guidance to the ASME Board on Professional Practice and Ethics on the Code of Ethics of Engineers.

1. Engineers shall hold paramount the safety, health, and welfare of the public in the performance of their professional duties.
    a. Engineers shall recognize that the lives, safety, health, and welfare of the general public are dependent upon engineering judgments, decisions and practices incorporated into structures, machines, products, processes and devices.
    b. Engineers shall not approve or seal plans and/or specifications that are not of a design safe to the public health and welfare and in conformity with accepted engineering standards.
    c. Whenever the Engineers' professional judgments are overruled under circumstances where the safety, health, and welfare of the public are endangered, the Engineers shall inform their clients and/or employers of the possible consequences.
        i.   Engineers shall endeavor to provide data such as published standards, test codes, and quality control procedures that will enable the users to understand safe use during life expectancy associated with the designs, products, or systems for which they are responsible.
        ii. Engineers shall conduct reviews of the safety and reliability of the designs, products, or systems for which they are responsible before giving their approval to the plans for the design.
        iii. Whenever Engineers observe conditions, directly related to their employment, which they believe will endanger public safety or health, they shall inform the proper authority of the situation.
    d. If engineers have knowledge of or reason to believe that another person or firm may be in violation of any of the provisions of these Canons, they shall present such information to the proper authority in writing and shall cooperate with the proper authority in furnishing such further information or assistance as may be required.

2. Engineers shall perform services only in areas of their competence.
    a. Engineers shall undertake to perform engineering assignments only when qualified by education and/or experience in the specific technical field of engineering involved.
    b. Engineers may accept an assignment requiring education and/or experience outside of their own fields of competence, but their services shall be restricted to other phases of the project in which they are qualified associates, consultants, or employees.

3. Engineers shall continue their professional development throughout their careers, and should provide opportunities for the professional and ethical development of those engineers under their supervision.

4. Engineers shall act in professional matters for each employer or client as faithful agents or trustees, and shall avoid conflicts of interest or the appearance of conflicts of interest.
    a. Engineers shall avoid all known conflicts of interest with their employers or clients and shall promptly inform their employers or clients of any business association, interests, or circumstances, which could influence their judgment or the quality of their services.
    b. Engineers shall not undertake any assignments which would knowingly create a potential conflict of interest between themselves and their clients or their employers.
    c. Engineers shall not accept compensation, financial or otherwise, from more than one party for services on the same project, or for services pertaining to the same project, unless the circumstances are fully disclosed to , and agreed to, by all interested parties.
    d. Engineers shall not solicit or accept financial or other valuable considerations, for specifying products or material or equipment suppliers, without disclosure to their clients or employers.
    e. Engineers shall not solicit or accept gratuities, directly or indirectly, from contractors, their agents, or other parties dealing with their clients or employers in connection with work for which they are responsible. Where official public policy or employers' policies tolerate acceptance of modest gratuities or gifts, engineers shall avoid a conflict of interest by complying with appropriate policies and shall avoid the appearance of a conflict of interest.
    f. When in public service as members, advisors, or employees of a governmental body or department, Engineers shall not

participate in considerations or actions with respect to services provided by them or their organization(s) in private or product engineering practice.

g. Engineers shall not solicit an engineering contract from a governmental body or other entity on which a principal, officer, or employee of their organization serves as a member without disclosing their relationship and removing themselves from any activity of the body which concerns their organization.

h. Engineers working on codes, standards or governmental sanction rules and specifications shall exercise careful judgment in their determinations to ensure a balanced viewpoint, and avoid a conflict of interest.

i. When, as a result of their studies, Engineers believe a project(s) will not be successful, they shall so advise their employer or client.

j. Engineers shall treat information coming to them in the course of their assignments as confidential, and shall not user such information as a means of making personal profit if such action is adverse to the interests of their clients, their employers or the public.

    i. They will not disclose confidential information concerning the business affairs or technical processes of any present or former employer or client or bidder under evaluation, without his consent, unless required by law or court order.

    ii. They shall not reveal confidential information or finding of any commission or board of which they are members unless required by law or court order.

    iii. Designs supplied to Engineers by clients shall not be duplicated by the Engineers for others without the express permission of the client(s).

k. Engineers shall act with fairness and justice to all parties when administering a construction (or other) contract.

l. Before undertaking work for others in which Engineers may make improvements, plans, designs, inventions, or other records which may justify seeking copyrights, patents, or proprietary rights, Engineers shall enter into positive agreements regarding the rights of respective parties.

m. Engineers shall admit their own errors when proven wrong and refrain from distorting or altering the facts to justify their mistakes or decisions.

n. Engineers shall not accept professional employment or assignments outside of their regular work without the knowledge of their employers.

o. Engineers shall not attempt to attract an employee from other employers or from the market place by false or misleading representations.

5. Engineers shall build their professional reputation on the merit of their services and shall not compete unfairly with others.
    a. Engineers shall negotiate contracts for professional services on the basis of demonstrated competence and qualifications for the type of professional service required.
    b. Engineers shall not request, propose, or accept professional commissions on a contingent basis if, under the circumstances, their professional judgments may be compromised.
    c. Engineers shall not falsify or permit misrepresentation of their, or their associates', academic or professional qualification. They shall not misrepresent or exaggerate their degrees of responsibility in or for the subject matter of prior assignments. Brochures or other presentations used to solicit personal employment shall not misrepresent pertinent facts concerning employers, employees, associates, joint venturers, or their accomplishments.
    d. Engineers shall prepare articles for the lay or technical press which are only factual. Technical Communications for publication (theses, articles, papers, reports, etc.) which are based on research involving more than one individual (including students or supervising faculty, industrial supervisor/researcher or other co-workers) must recognize all significant contributors. Plagiarism, the act of substantially using another's ideas or written materials without due credit, is unethical.
    e. Engineers shall not maliciously or falsely, directly or indirectly, injure the professional reputation, prospects, practice, or employment of another engineer, nor shall they indiscriminately criticize another's work.
    f. Engineers shall not use equipment, supplies, laboratory or office facilities of their employers to carry on outside private practice without consent.

6. Engineers shall associate only with reputable persons or organizations.
    a. Engineers shall not knowingly associate with or permit the use of their names or firm names in business ventures by any person or firm which they know, or have reason to believe, are engaging in business or professional practices of a fraudulent or dishonest nature.
    b. Engineers shall not use association with non-engineers,

corporations, or partnerships to disguise unethical acts.

7. Engineers shall issue public statements only in an objective and truthful manner.
    a. Engineers shall endeavor to extend public knowledge and to prevent misunderstandings of the achievements of engineering.
    b. Engineers shall be completely objective and truthful in all professional reports, statements or testimony. They shall include all relevant and pertinent information in such reports, statements or testimony.
    c. Engineers, when serving as expert or technical witnesses before any court, commission, or other tribunal, shall express an engineering opinion only when it is founded on their adequate knowledge of the facts in issue, their background of technical competence in the subject matter, and their belief in the accuracy and propriety of their testimony.
    d. Engineers shall issue no statements, criticisms, or arguments on engineering matters which are inspired or paid for by an interested party or parties on whose behalf they are speaking, and by revealing the existence of any financial interest they may have in matters under discussion.
    e. Engineers shall be truthful in explaining their work and merit, and shall avoid any act tending to promote their own interest at the expense of the integrity and honor of the profession or another individual.

8. Engineers accepting membership in The American Society of Mechanical Engineers by this action agree to abide by this Society Policy on Ethics and procedures for its implementation.

APPENDIX 3: AMERICAN SOCIETY OF CIVIL ENGINEERS CODE OF ETHICS[11]

American Society of Civil Engineers (ASCE)
Code of Ethics

Adopted September 25, 1976
Amended October 25, 1980 and April 17, 1993
Effective January 1, 1977

Fundamental Principles

Engineers uphold and advance the integrity, honor, and dignity of the engineering profession by:

1. Using their knowledge and skill for the enhancement of human welfare;
2. Being honest and impartial and serving with fidelity the public, their employers and clients:
3. Striving to increase the competence and prestige of the engineering profession; and
4. Supporting the professional and technical societies of their disciplines.

Fundamental Canons

1. Engineers shall hold paramount the safety, health, and welfare of the public in the performance of their professional duties.
2. Engineers shall perform services only in areas of their competence.
3. Engineers shall issue public statements only in an objective and truthful manner.
4. Engineers shall act in professional matters for each employer or client as faithful agents or trustees, and shall avoid conflicts of interest.
5. Engineers shall build their professional reputation on the merit of their services and shall not compete unfairly with others.
6. Engineers shall act in such a manner as to uphold and enhance the honor, integrity, and dignity of the engineering profession.
7. Engineers shall continue their professional development throughout their careers, and hsall provide opportunities for the professional development of those engineers under their supervision.

ASCE Guidelines to Practice
Under the Fundamental Canons of Ethics

CANON 1. Engineers shall hold paramount the safety, health, and welfare of the public in the performance of their professional duties.

    a. Engineers shall recognize that the lives, safety, health, and welfare of the general public are dependent upon engineering judgments, decisions and practices incorporated into structures, machines, products, processes and devices.

    b. Engineers shall approve or seal only those design documents, reviewed or prepared by them, which are determined to be safe for public health and welfare in conformity with accepted engineering standards.

    c. Engineers whose professional judgment is overruled under circumstances where the safety, health, and welfare of the public are endangered, shall inform their clients or employers of the possible consequences.

    d. Engineers who have knowledge or reason to believe that another person or firm may be in violation of any of the provisions of Canon I shall present such information to the proper authority in writing and shall cooperate with the proper authority in furnishing such further information or assistance as may be required.

    e. Engineers should seek opportunities to be of constructive service in civic affairs and work for the advancement of the safety, health and well being of their communities.

    f. Engineers should be committed to improving the environment to enhance the quality of life.

CANON 2. Engineers shall perform services only in areas of their competence.

    a. Engineers shall undertake to perform engineering assignments only when qualified by education or experience in the technical field of engineering involved.

    b. Engineers may accept an assignment requiring education or experience outside of their own fields of competence, provided their services are restricted to those phases of the project in which they are qualified. All other phases of such project shall be performed by qualified associates, consultants, or employees.

    c. Engineers shall not affix their signatures or seals to any engineering plan or document dealing with subject matter in which they lack competence by virtue of education or experience or to any such plan or document not reviewed or prepared under their supervisory control.

CANON 3. Engineers shall issue public statements only in an objective and truthful manner.

a. Engineers should endeavor to extend the public knowledge of engineering and sustainable development, and shall not participate in the dissemination of untrue, unfair or exaggerated statements regarding engineering.

b. Engineers shall be objective and truthful in professional reports, statements, or testimony. They shall include all relevant and pertinent information in such reports, statements, or testimony.

c. Engineers, when serving as expert witnesses, shall express an engineering opinion only when it is founded upon adequate knowledge of the facts, upon a background of technical competence, and upon honest conviction.

d. Engineers shall issue no statements, criticisms, or arguments on engineering matters which are inspired or paid for by interested parties, unless they indicate on whose behalf the statements are made.

e. Engineers shall be dignified and modest in explaining their work and merit, and will avoid any act tending to promote their own interests at the expense of the integrity, honor and dignity of the profession.

CANON 4. Engineers shall act in professional matters for each employer or client as faithful agents or trustees, and shall avoid conflicts of interest.

a. Engineers shall avoid all known or potential conflicts of interest with their employers or clients and shall promptly inform their employers or clients of any business association, interests, or circumstances which could influence their judgment or the quality of their services.

b. Engineers shall not accept compensation from more than one party for services on the same project, or for services pertaining to the same project, unless the circumstances are fully disclosed to and agreed to, by all interested parties.

c. Engineers shall not solicit or accept gratuities, directly or indirectly, from contractors, their agents, or other parties dealing with their clients or employers in connection with work for which they are responsible.

d. Engineers in public service as members, advisors, or employees of a governmental body or department shall not participate in considerations or actions with respect to services solicited or provided by them or their organization in private or public engineering practice.

e. Engineers shall advise their employers or clients when, as a result of their studies, they believe a project will not be successful.

f. Engineers shall not use confidential information coming to them in the course of their assignments as a means of making personal profit if such action is adverse to the interests of their clients, employers or the public.

g. Engineers shall not accept professional employment outside of their regular work or interest without the knowledge of their employers.

CANON 5. Engineers shall build their professional reputation on the merit of their services and shall not compete unfairly with others.

a. Engineers shall not give, solicit or receive either directly or indirectly, any political contribution, gratuity, or unlawful consideration in order to secure work, exclusive of securing salaried positions through employment agencies.

b. Engineers should negotiate contracts for professional services fairly and on the basis of demonstrated competence and qualifications for the type of professional service required.

c. Engineers may request, propose or accept professional commissions on a contingent basis only under circumstances in which their professional judgments would not be compromised.

d. Engineers shall not falsify or permit misrepresentation of their academic or professional qualifications or experience.

e. Engineers shall give proper credit for engineering work to those to whom credit is due, and shall recognize the proprietary interests of others. Whenever possible, they shall name the person or persons who may be responsible for designs, inventions, writings or other accomplishments.

f. Engineers may advertise professional services in a way that does not contain misleading language or is in any other manner derogatory to the dignity of the profession. Examples of permissible advertising are as follows:

    i.   Professional cards in recognized, dignified publications, and listings in rosters or directories published by responsible organizations, provided that the cards or listings are consistent in size and content and are in a section of the publication regularly devoted to such professional cards.

    ii. Brochures which factually describe experience, facilities, personnel and capacity to render service, providing they are not misleading with respect to the engineer's participation in projects described.

    iii. Display advertising in recognized dignified business and professional publications, providing it is factual and is not misleading with respect to the engineer's extent of participation in projects described.

    iv. A statement of the engineers' names or the name of the firm and statement of the type of service posted on projects for which they render services.

    v.   Preparation or authorization of descriptive articles for the lay or technical press, which are factual and dignified. Such articles shall not imply anything more than direct participation in the project described.

vi. Permission by engineers for their names to be used in commercial advertisements, such as may be published by contractors, material suppliers, etc., only by means of a modest, dignified notation acknowledging the engineers' participation in the project described. Such permission shall not include public endorsement of proprietary products.

g. Engineers shall not maliciously or falsely, directly or indirectly, injure the professional reputation, prospects, practice or employment of another engineer or indiscriminately criticize another's work.

h. Engineers shall not use equipment, supplies, laboratory or office facilities of their employers to carry on outside private practice without the consent of their employers.

CANON 6. Engineers shall act in such a manner as to uphold and enhance the honor, integrity, and dignity of the engineering profession and shall act with zero tolerance for bribery, fraud, and corruption.

a. Engineers shall not knowingly engage in business or professional practices of a fraudulent, dishonest or unethical nature.

b. Engineers shall be scrupulously honest in their control and spending of monies, and promote effective use of resources through open, honest and impartial service with fidelity to the public, employers, associates and clients.

c. Engineers shall act with zero-tolerance for bribery, fraud, and corruption in all engineering or construction activities in which they are engaged.

d. Engineers should be especially vigilant to maintain appropriate ethical behavior where payments of gratuities or bribes are institutionalized practices.

e. Engineers should strive for transparency in the procurement and execution of projects. Transparency includes disclosure of names, addresses, purposes, and fees or commissions paid for all agents facilitating projects.

f. Engineers should encourage the use of certifications specifying zero tolerance for bribery, fraud, and corruption in all contracts.

CANON 7. Engineers shall continue their professional development throughout their careers, and shall provide opportunities for the professional development of those engineers under their supervision.

a. Engineers should keep current in their specialty fields by engaging in professional practice, participating in continuing education courses, reading in the technical literature, and attending professional meetings and seminars.

b. Engineers should encourage their engineering employees to become registered at the earliest possible date.

c. Engineers should encourage engineering employees to attend and present papers at professional and technical society meetings.

d. Engineers shall uphold the principle of mutually satisfying relationships between employers and employees with respect to terms of employment including professional grade descriptions, salary ranges, and fringe benefits.

APPENDIX 4: INSTITUTE FOR INDUSTRIAL ENGINEERING CODE OF ETHICS[12]

IIE endorses the Canon of Ethics provided by the Accreditation Board for Engineering and Technology.

The Fundamental Principles

Engineers uphold and advance the integrity, honor, and dignity of the engineering profession by:
1. Using their knowledge and skill for the enhancement of human welfare;
2. Being honest and impartial, and serving with fidelity the public, their employers and clients;
3. Striving to increase the competence and prestige of the engineering profession; and
4. Supporting the professional and technical societies of their disciplines.

The Fundamental Canons

1) Engineers shall hold paramount the safety, health and welfare of the public in the performance of their professional duties.
2) Engineers shall perform services only in the areas of their competence.
3) Engineers shall issue public statements only in an objective and truthful manner.
4) Engineers shall act in professional matters for each employer or client as faithful agents or trustees, and shall avoid conflicts of interest.
5) Engineers shall build their professional reputation on the merit of their services and shall not compete unfairly with others.
6) Engineers shall associate only with reputable persons or organizations.
7) Engineers shall continue their professional development throughout their careers and shall provide opportunities for the professional development of those engineers under their supervision.

APPENDIX 5: AMERICAN INSTITUTE OF AERONAUTICS AND ASTRONAUTICS[13]

AIAA Code of Ethics

PRECEPT
The AIAA Member to uphold and advance the honor and dignity of the aerospace profession and in keeping with high standards of ethical conduct:

I. Will be honest and impartial, and will serve with devotion his employer and the public;
II. Will strive to increase the competence and prestige of the aerospace profession;
III. Will use his knowledge and skill for the advancement of human welfare.

RELATIONS WITH THE PUBLIC
1.1 The AIAA member will have proper regard for the safety, health, and welfare of the public in the performance of his professional duties.
1.2 The member will endeavor to extend public knowledge and appreciation of aerospace science and its achievements.
1.3 The member will be dignified and modest in explaining his work and merit and will ever uphold the honor and dignity of his profession.
1.4 The member will express an opinion on a professional subject only when it is founded on adequate knowledge and honest conviction.
1.5 The member will preface any ex parte statement, criticisms, or arguments that he may issue by clearly indicating on whose behalf they are made.

RELATIONS WITH EMPLOYERS AND CLIENTS
2.1 The AIAA member will act in professional matters as a faithful agent or trustee for each employer or client.
2.2 The member will act fairly and justly toward vendors and contractors, and will not accept from vendors or contractors any commissions or allowances which represent a conflict of interest.
2.3 The member will inform his employer or client if he is financially interested in any vendor or contractor, or in any invention, machines, or apparatus, which is involved in a project or work of his employer or client. The member will not allow such interest to affect his decision regarding services which he may be called upon to perform.
2.4 The member will indicate to his employer or client the adverse

consequences to be expected if his judgment is overruled.

2.5   The member will undertake only those professional assignments for which he is qualified. The member will engage or advise his employer or client to engage specialists and will cooperate with them whenever his employer's or client's interests are served best by such an arrangement.

2.6   The member will not disclose information concerning the business affairs or technical processes of any present or former employer or client without his consent.

2.7   The member will not accept compensation, financial or otherwise, from more than one party for the same service, or for other services pertaining to the same work, without the consent of all interested parties.

2.8   The member will report to his employer or client any matters within his area of expertise which the member believes represent a contravention of public law, regulation, health or safety.

RELATIONS WITH OTHER PROFESSIONALS

3.1   The AIAA member will take care that credit for professional work is given to those to whom credit is properly due.

3.2   The member will provide a prospective employee with complete information on working conditions and his proposed status of employment, and after employment will keep him informed of any changes in them.

3.3   The member will uphold the principle of appropriate and adequate compensation for those engaged in professional work, including those in subordinate capacities.

3.4   The member will endeavor to provide opportunity for the professional development and advancement of those in his employ or under his supervision.

3.5   The member will not injure maliciously the professional reputation, prospects, or practice of another professional.

3.6   The member will cooperate in advancing the aerospace profession by interchanging information and experience with other professionals and students, and by contributing to public communication media, to the efforts of engineering and scientific societies and schools.

CODE ADMINISTRATION

Establish a three-member Ethical Conduct Panel (ECP) reporting to the Board of Directors to:

- Review all complaints, recommendations, criticism of, and questions concerning a code of ethics for all AIAA members and insure the privacy of all inquiries.
- By unanimous vote recommend a course of action merited by the applicant.

- Where appropriate, present the ECP recommendations to the AIAA Board of Directors for approval and implementation.
- Report to each regular AIAA Board of Directors' meeting the disposition of all cases, including decisions not to act, received by the ECP in the period preceding each meeting.

The Ethical Conduct Panel (ECP) will consist of three AIAA members selected by the Board of Directors. A member will serve for three years. One member will be appointed each year to provide two-thirds member continuity. If a member of ECP disqualifies himself or herself the board shall appoint a replacement.

References

Fasching, D.J. *The Ethical Challenge of Auschwitz and Hiroshima: Apocalypse or Utopia?* State University of New York Press, Albany, NY, 1993.

Fleddermann, C.B. and Fleddermann, C.B., *Engineering Ethics,* Prentice-Hall, Inc., 1999.

Frankena, W.K. *Ethics*, 2nd ed. Englewood Cliffs, N.J.: Prentice-Hall, Inc., 1973.

Johnson, D.G., ed. *Ethical Issues in Engineering.* Englewood, N.J.: Prentice-Hall, Inc., 1991.

Harris, C.E., Jr., Davis,M., Pritchard, M.S., and Rabins, M.J. "Engineering Ethics: What? Why? How? And When?" Journal of Engineering Education, April 1996, pp. 93-96.

Herkert, J.R., "*ABET's Engineering Criteria 2000 and Engineering Ethics: Where Do We Go From Here?,"* International Conference on Ethics in Engineering and Computer Science, Case Western Reserve University, 1999. Martin, M. W., and Schinzinger, R. *Ethics in Engineering.* New York: McGraw-Hill, 1996.

Pinkus, R.L.B. (Editor), Shuman, L., and Hummon, N.P. *Engineering Ethics: Balancing Cost, Schedule, and Risk– Lessons Learned From the Space Shuttle.* New York: Cambridge University Press, 1997.

Schlossberger, E. *The Ethical Engineer.* Philadelphia: Temple University Press, 1993.

Stevenson, J.T. *Engineering Ethics: Practices and Principles.* Toronto: Canadian Scholars' Press, 1987.

Wells, P., Hardy J., and Davis, M., *Conflicts of Interest in Engineering,* Dubuque, Iowa: Kendall/Hunt Publishing Company, 1986.

Whitbeck, C. and Flowers, W.C., *Ethics in Engineering Practice and Research,* Cambridge University Press, 1998.

Velasquez, M., Andre,C., Shanks, S.J., and Meyer, M.J. "Thinking Ethically: A Framework for Moral Decision Making" *Issues in Ethics.* http://www.scu.edu/Ethics/practicing/decision/thinking.shtml. 17 May 1998.

CODES OF ETHICS

AIAA Code of Ethics. Online. AAIA. Available: http://www.aiaa.org/information/ethics.html. 14 May 1998.

ASCE Code of Ethics. Online. WWW Ethics Center. Available: http://www.cwru.edu/affil/wwwethics/codes/ASCEcode.html. 14 May 1998.

ASME Code of Ethics. Online. ASMENet. Available: http://www.asme.org/asme/policies/p15-7.html. 14 May 1998.

IEEE Code of Ethics. Online. WWW Ethics Center. Available: http://www.cwru.edu/affil/wwwethics/codes/IEEEcode.html. 14 May 1998.

IIE Engineering Code of Ethics. Online. IIE. Available: http://www.iienet.org/code_of_ethics.htm. 14 May 1998.

NSPE Code of Ethics for Engineers: Engineer's Creed. Online. NSPE Online. Available: http://www.nspe.org/eh-home.htm. 14 May 1998.

NSPE Code of Ethics for Engineers. Online. NSPE Online. Available: http://www.nspe.org/eh1-code.htm. 14 May 1998.

---

[1] The material in this chapter was originally created by Akila McConnell.
[2] *ibid.* p. 51.
[3] J.T. Stevenson. Engineering Ethics: Practices and Principles. (Toronto: Canadian Scholars' Press, 1987): 50-51
[4] http://en.wikipedia.org/wiki/Socrates, 2005.
[5] http://www.m-w.com/cgi-bin/dictionary
[6] *ibid*, p. 58
[7] http://www.gene.com/ae/21st/SER/BE/definitions.html
[8] http://www.cwru.edu/affil/wwwethics/glossary.html
[9] http://www.nspe.org/eh1-code.htm
[10] From http://www.asme.org/work/frames/frame_courses.htm
[11] From http://www.cwru.edu/affil/wwwethics/codes/ASCEcode.html
[12] From http://www.iienet.org/code_of_ethics.htm
[13] From http://www.aiaa.org/information/ethics.html

5 Engineering Design Principles

LEARNING GOALS

- Explain the importance of engineering design in solving real-world problems
- Show how product design impacts Society
- Draw a flowchart that explains the design process
- Describe each element of the design process
- Illustrate each element with an example
- Implement the design process in the development of an actual product
- Identify how errors in implementing the design process might cause major problems/accidents

5.1 INTRODUCTION[1]

Design is a central activity in engineering. Design problems are typically open-ended and ill-structured. That is, there are usually many acceptable solutions and the solutions cannot normally be found by routinely applying a mathematical formula in a structured way (Dym, 1994). Design, as is traditionally taught, requires the use of subjects that help in analyzing the problem such as dimensioning, calculating heat transfer, and determining velocities. In the real world, this traditional material, analysis, is only a part of the design engineers' job. Engineers have to perform both engineering and management work by considering factors such as cost, schedule, risk, and safety. Engineers must also work with people both within and outside their organization to bring the design to fruition (Ertas and Jones, 1996). They typically use engineering drawings, text, templates, or models to communicate their design ideas to the people within and outside their organization (AT&T, 1993). In the real-world, if the design specifications are wrong, the company's profits suffer or more importantly, people may be injured or die.

---

[1] The material in this chapter was originally created by Justin Cochran.

> **Engineering Design (Definition):** This is the process of devising a system, component, or process to meet desired needs. It is a decision making process (often iterative), in which the basic sciences, mathematics, and engineering sciences are applied to convert resources optimally to meet a stated objective. Among the fundamental elements of the design process are the establishment of objectives and criteria, synthesis, analysis, construction, testing, and evaluation... It is essential to include a variety of realistic constraints such as economic factors, safety, reliability, aesthetics, ethics, and social impact.
>
> Accreditation Board for Engineering and Technology (ABET, 1996).

5.2 ELEMENTS OF THE DESIGN PROCESS

Design has been a characteristic of human endeavor as shown by the primitive societies making basic implements or making shelters (Dym, 1994). In the past, "designing" was inextricably linked with the "making" of the primitive implements - that is there was no separate, discernible modeling process. This approach to design is a distinguishing feature of a craft. In contrast, an engineering designer does not, typically, produce the final end-product; rather, he/she produces a set of fabrication specifications for that product. The specification has to be such that the fabricator can make the product in question without talking to the designer (Dym, 1994). Thus, the specification has to be both complete and specific; there should be no ambiguity and nothing can be left out.

> **Example of Importance of Design:** The 1981 collapse of Kansas City's Hyatt Regency Hotel occurred because a contractor, unable to procure threaded rods sufficiently long to suspend a second-floor walkway from a roof truss, hung it instead from a fourth-floor walkway, using shorter rods. The supports of the fourth-floor walkway were not designed to carry the second-floor walkway in addition to its own dead and live loads.
>
> During a tea dance in the lobby in 1981, the walkways were crowded with spectators. The load these people placed on the structure proved to be too much, and the nuts under the top walkway were pulled through the walkway structure. The bottom walkway crashed to the ground and the top walkway fell onto it. In total, 114 people died and over 200 were injured, in what is now considered one of the worst structural tragedies in the United States.
>
> Had the designer been able to talk with a fabricator while the design was in progress, he would have learned that no one manufactured that rod in the lengths needed to hang the second-floor walkway from the roof truss.
>
> Source: http://www.taknosys.com/ethics/cases/ec02.htm

Thus, design is a primary component of product development. The attention given to a product during the design stage has a direct bearing on the future costs and performance of a product. Without time and money invested in the initial stages of a product's life, the costs associated with failure escalate. The power of design to predict and correct failures before their occurrence has led many corporations to invest great amounts of manpower and money in the early design phases.

Engineering students must understand that design is one of the primary tasks that engineers encounter. Design is expected to take as much as 30% of an engineer's time on the job (National Research Council, 1983, 1999). If the engineer's position is not purely a design position, design skills are still needed in order to make effective decisions.

Furthermore, it is important for engineers to design good products. Management often does not understand the role of designers either. Traditionally there was little way to determine the value of different design alternatives. The communication between designer and management must improve for engineers to design profitably. Also, designers must be trained to keep pace with technology so that they maintain or enhance their value to the company. The design process is becoming a lot more complex. For example, Boeing designed its 777 aircraft in a paper-less mode. Boeing integrated its Computer Aided Design (CAD) systems so that the 777 design team could access them from anywhere in the world and create virtual mock-ups instead of physical mock-ups. Boeing distributed 2,200 computer terminals to its overall 777 design team. The terminals were connected to, one of the largest grouping of IBM mainframe computers in the world. This provided key

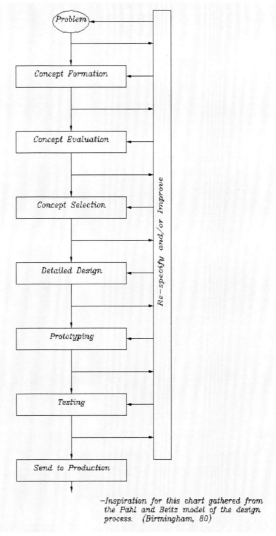

−Inspiration for this chart gathered from the Pahl and Beitz model of the design process. (Birmingham, 80)

Figure 11: Elements of the Design

116

participants in the design process, ranging from airframe manufacturers in Japan, to engine manufacturers in the U.K. and U.S., immediate access to the data. The systems also allowed all involved in the process to be aware of changes as they were made and confirmed. The changed design process allowed Boeing to cut its traditional 60 months development time to less than 48 months (Condit, 1994; Snyder, et al., 1998).

Simply designing a product is often not good enough anymore. Design has to be iterated often to improve quality and reduce costs. The safety of a product must be considered, as should public opinion. If design is not taken seriously, products will not sell, businesses will collapse, and competitors will thrive. To compete with others in this economy, good design must prevail as an iterative tool of continuous improvement.

A graphical concept of a design approach is shown in Figure 11. As can be seen, design is an iterative process and consists of distinct steps. We will explain each of the steps below and use the example of the design-build-manufacture of the Boeing 777 aircraft to illustrate the concepts.

5.2.1 Problem Definition

Product design typically arises from a need or a problem. Every manmade thing around you likely originated from this point. The automobile filled a need for transportation. The light bulb filled the need for light on demand. Shoes filled the need for foot comfort. Some items around you fix a single problem, while others, a multitude of problems. Automobiles transport both people and equipment for many different purposes (e.g. passenger cars, fire trucks, military vehicles). No matter what the product is, it is likely that its beginnings are rooted in solving a problem.

In defining a problem, care must be taken in defining the specifications of the problem. Critical characteristics, or constraints, must be determined. For example, if you are asked to design a car navigation system, you may find that an ideal location for the driver's view is the dash of the car. However, the navigation system might be too large for the dashboard. Therefore, steps must be taken to reduce the size of the navigation system or relocate pieces of it to other areas of the vehicle. Criteria such as physical size constraints must be specified so that you can work with the manufacturers of the car navigation system so as to reduce the size of the system.

For Boeing, the problem was defined by its competitors. During 1990, the leaders in the commercial airplane industry were Boeing, Airbus Industrie, and McDonnell Douglas. In 1986, Airbus and McDonnell

Douglas were building new planes - the A-330/340 and MD-11/12 - to carry between 300 and 400 passengers. Airbus and McDonnell-Douglas had modified their internal systems and were effectively producing new products in a shorter developmental cycle than Boeing. Both were using new techniques and procedures, leveraged with the use of telecommunications in an attempt to erode Boeing's dominant position in the marketplace. These planes were designed for airlines that wanted to fill the gap between the 200 passengers that a Boeing *767* could carry and 425 passengers that a Boeing *747* could carry. In 1992, United Airlines placed a multibillion-dollar order with Airbus instead of Boeing, its historical supplier. Boeing was forced to design the Boeing *777* to fill the gap in demand and to cover the market for aircraft carrying between 300

Saving the Baby Bird – A Classroom Example

A baby bird, too young to take care of himself, has fallen out of a tree in your yard. Can you find a way to save the bird? Perhaps the Engineering Design Process can assist us.

Problem Definition – A baby bird has fallen from its nest in my yard. I need to determine a solution to safely return the bird to its nest.

Constraints
- Human hands cannot touch the bird or its mother will reject it.
- The nest is 15 feet from the ground.
- The bird should arrive safely in its nest within two hours of its fall.
- The baby bird is too young to survive on its own.
- *Enter your own…*

5.2.2 Concept Formation

Once a need or a problem has been established, concepts for products that fill the need or correct the problem must be developed. This is usually the point where the technical aspects of engineering takes center stage. The concepts that are learned in physics and chemistry, mathematics, and science-based engineering courses must be creatively applied to solving the problem. After all, product design is a creative activity (if not purely creative, a creative use of existing knowledge). The engineer's imagination is an essential aspect of new product design or design improvement. Exercising and developing creativity in the mind enables one to efficiently accomplish new design tasks.

Using the engineering sciences developed over the years by our ancestors, we can use our knowledge of various theories in electricity, dynamics, thermodynamics, chemistry, particle physics, etc. to create solutions to problems. Ideas for solving problems may develop in unlikely places such as the shower or unlikely times such as while you sleep. More reliable methods exist, however, for conceiving ideas. Brainstorming is an extremely useful tool for idea generation. It allows a team of people to rapidly suggest ideas in a manner that inspires members of the team. Behavioral rules are necessary, though, to ensure the best possible brainstorming conditions.

Crucial to the brainstorming atmosphere is a positive outlook by the team members. Members must be willing to hear any idea, no matter the absurdity, and not evaluate merit or comment negatively about it. This creates an atmosphere of encouragement and acceptance. For the most productive sessions, everyone must feel welcome to participate.

Also important is that no idea should be evaluated in detail during the session. Elaborating on details can stifle the "momentum" of brainstorming. After the session, there will be opportunity to expand the details and evaluate the feasibility of an idea.

To aid in productive brainstorming, a facilitator, or session coordinator, should be chosen to stop negativity or idea development when they begin. Also, establishing a sequence around the room will allow everyone to speak and offset the overpowering members of the group. Members can either suggest an idea or pass. The facilitator should also stimulate the session so that a variety of ideas are present rather than one approach.

Finally, ideas must be captured. Videotapes, audiotapes, or written notes will suffice, if the ideas are presented clearly. Note that clear presentation of an idea does not mean that details need to be presented. Captured ideas will be available for evaluation at another time.

5.2.3 Concept Evaluation

Upon developing some ideas for solving a problem, these ideas must be reduced in number based on feasibility. Product feasibility is affected by many factors including costs, technological limitations, legal limitations, environmental impacts, and time. This is an important time to try to estimate the value of the solutions the team has conceived. Without some estimation of how much money the company can earn

Mobile Phones

AT&T conceived the idea of car phones during the 1960s and sold this service to consumers. The overall demand was low since the product was bulky and took a lot of space in the front and trunk of a car. The company withdrew the product during the late 1960s.

By the 1990s, wireless phones had become compact and could be held in the palm of a hand. The prices decreased drastically and consumers started to use them a lot more. The miniaturization of circuits and advances in processors has made the hand-held wireless phone a technical possibility.

from the product, many ideas will not be excluded, as they should. For example, a company may estimate that a new product design could generate revenues of $1 million over its lifetime. If it costs more than $10 million to produce during its lifetime, then the net return on the product will be -$9 million and the idea is not currently feasible. In other instances, certain technologies may need to be developed before the product can be made economically. The costs associated with research and development of the technology may exceed the value of the product. However, an idea that was conceived years ago might become economically viable with new technology and can benefit the company now.

Saving the Baby Bird – A Classroom Example

Concept Evaluation:
- Slingshot the bird back into the nest
  - Low likelihood of returning the bird safely
- Throw the bird back into the nest
  - Low likelihood of returning the bird safely
- Climb the tree and place the bird back into the nest
  - Maybe with new gloves and a pouch, one could climb the tree (assuming one has that ability) and return the bird while under attack from the bird's mother
- Chop down the tree
  - Does not result in a safe return
- Leave the bird for the cat
  - Does not result in a safe return
- Use the "Beam" from "Star Trek"
  - Exceeds the scope of current technology
- Construct a basket/pole device to place the bird back in the nest
  - Maybe with the right construction and steady hands, might need some construction time and materials
- Call Animal Control or the Fire Department
  - Animal Control is not likely to respond, nor will the Fire Department in mast cases
- Build a pulley system
  - Likely requires climbing the tree for proper placement of pulleys to result in return to the nest, would be inferior to concept of climbing the tree and placing by hand
- Construct a birdhouse for the bird
  - Will not result in a safe return to the nest
- Use a ladder to climb the tree and place the bird back in the nest
  - Might be superior to climbing the tree without a ladder, might free a hand to carry the bird with gloves or basket, Is there a ladder available?

5.2.4 Concept Selection and Detailed Design

Once several feasible ideas have been evaluated, the best concepts are selected. Concept selection will typically be a group decision by management based on the evaluation materials produced by engineering, sales, and marketing. Then, the product typically enters a detailed design stage. Time is spent determining the specific characteristics of each piece of the product. These specifications are typically communicated through engineering drawings and specification sheets. In the not so distant past, drawings were hand drawn with pencil and paper, but in recent years the standard has become computer aided design (CAD). CAD software typically includes the capability to draw in two dimensions and label dimensions (Figure 12).

More sophisticated CAD packages will allow three dimensional and solid modeling. Solid modeling has many benefits, which become more important with increasing product complexity. A few of the benefits are: a) pieces can be assembled to determine interference, b) the drawing can be rotated and viewed from all angles, and c) material properties can be assigned to pieces for further engineering analysis and simulation. It is imperative that the engineering student becomes comfortable with CAD software for today's job market. The future engineer should note also that information technology (IT) is linking departments of companies together electronically in better ways that were awkward before. For example, Boeing used IT to reduce their design time for the 777 by linking engineering, accounting, suppliers, customers, communications, and management together through a common information system. Boeing also avoided creating a physical prototype for this project, a bold and unorthodox step for Boeing (Snyder et al., 1998). Boeing

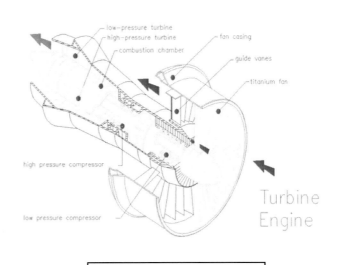

Figure 12: CAD Drawing

used two CAD systems, Computer graphics Aided Three-Dimensional Interactive Application (CATIA) and Electronic Preassembly In the Computer (EPIC) in order to automate its design processes.

CATIA was used to design specific components and was based on a Dassault/IBM system that was introduced to Boeing in 1986. This system allowed engineers to design components in three dimensions and ensured that they would properly fit and operate before they were physically produced. Use of the virtual mock-ups significantly reduced effort in systems integration for aircraft manufacture as compared to the use of physical mock-ups. Boeing Chief Project Engineer for digital product design, Dick Johnson, stated, "With the physical mock-ups we had three classes: class 1, class 2, and class 3. The engineer had three opportunities at three levels of detail to check his parts, and nothing in between. With CATIA, he can do it day in and day out over the whole development of the airplane, and so it's a tremendous advantage."

EPIC allowed the different components of the aircraft to be designed and integrated into a computer simulation of the whole plane. This was a system designed by Boeing for initial implementation in the *777* project. It allowed engineers to integrate all the systems on the aircraft to ensure that there were no interferences, and that all components interacted appropriately. Engineers using this system could view individual parts from varying perspectives, as well as operate the component as it was projected to be built. These components were then linked in a virtual mock-up for systems integration. The introduction of the EPIC system made possible a direct link between the computer description of the design of a component and the instructions that a machine tool would need to make it. This eliminated the earlier habit of "throwing the design over the wall" and letting production worry about creating the equipment.

The apparent freedom to change parts until they became final could have led to absolute confusion as engineers constantly "tinkered" with their systems. Boeing countered this by imposing periodic design "freezes," where engineers would be forced to resolve conflicts their parts or systems created with all other systems. Resolving conflicts was critical in the design of the rudder, fuselage doors, the fuselage, and engines, since all these components were produced by subcontractors, mainly outside the continental United States. For example, the rudder for the *777* was produced by ASTA in Australia, using Boeing carbon-fiber technology in a German-built autoclave. Changes in the rudder design had to be fed to ASTA in Melbourne to meet production deadlines in the United States. Analysis of the rudder design revealed that there would be some aerodynamic "flutter" requiring a change in the design of the component. ASTA's representative to the rudder design-build teams provided constant input to her parent company, allowing them to strive to meet production deadlines.

Although CATIA was expensive to introduce and initially cumbersome to use, the system helped Boeing eliminate 65 percent of change errors and rework, 15 percent better than the target set. CATIA also saved Boeing from having to make expensive engineering mock-ups of the 777 before it built the real aircraft (Guy, 1995). Digital mock-ups provided engineers with the physical reassurance of a design before they committed the design to production.

Saving the Baby Bird – A Classroom Example

Concept Selection:

It was pretty easy to narrow the list of ideas down to 3 or 4 based simply on their ability to solve our problem while meeting the constraints. Narrowing the list farther requires a more detailed assessment of the options. Our remaining options were:

- Climb the tree and place the bird back into the nest
- Construct a basket/pole device to place the bird back in the nest
- Use a ladder to climb the tree and place the bird back in the nest

Of these options the ladder solution appears to be the most economical under the conditions that you own a sufficient ladder and gloves or a basket. If the ladder is not available, then perhaps some thought must be given to your tree climbing skills, and the distance/strength of the tree branches. Finally, there are many different ways to construct a basket/pole device based on objects around the house. This might prove to be the most efficient if few materials need to be purchased or if a ladder is not available. Essentially, the concept selected will depend on the more stringent constraints of the environment that is being operated in and the availability of materials.

Detailed Design:

This Intro to Engineering class chose to use a ladder to solve our bird rescue problem. However, the class made the assumption that this was an effort of one person and that it would improve safety to place stakes at the base of the ladder to prevent slippage of the ladder at that elevation, especially if the climb was one handed.

5.2.5 Prototyping

With detailed drawings and specifications, the product can be submitted to the prototype stage. During prototyping, models (full-size and/or scaled) of the product are built to further determine the merit of the idea. Questions about the assumptions made about engineering theory, costs involved, construction time, etc. need to be answered. Often times, paper ideas leave out many details and address few of the problems associated with the physical construction of the product (this effect is greatly reduced with modern CAD software). If a product went directly from the drawing board to the production line without prototyping, the results may not be successful. Unlike full-scale production, prototyping allows the company to evaluate the product and discover problems inexpensively. With prototyping, if a design must be scrapped or modified, the cost is minimal as compared to attempting production and failing.

CATIA saved Boeing from having to make expensive engineering prototypes of the 777 before it built the real thing. Prototypes provide engineers with the physical reassurance of a design - allowing them to check that parts fit together properly and do not interfere with cable and wire runs - before they commit the design to production. Boeing actually did make one mock-up: the nose of the 777, to verify that digital pre-assembly would work.

5.2.6 Testing

Testing of prototypes is the next phase. Prototypes may go through several design iterations before the final prototypes. The final prototypes are built to be close to the target product. Characteristics such as appearance, materials, and performance will be matched closely with the expected production line item. To check product performance, testing must be conducted to ensure that the product meets explicit specifications. An extremely important point that is often left unstated is that a product's quality, or the ability of a product to meet specifications, cannot be judged without specifications. Any characteristic that is considered important must be stated or there is no standard to judge by. For example, the car navigation system's display may produce a glare at certain driver perspectives. A tilting display may enable a larger range of perspectives from the driver's position. This tilt angle must be specified as well as the expected perspectives of the driver depending on the person's size. During testing, the final prototype will be checked to see if it can achieve the specified angles to eliminate the glare problem. If the adjustments do not reduce the glare problem, the prototype must be redesigned or the specifications need to be reevaluated. The need for specifications continues into realms of physical performance as well, including product life, speed, power consumption, efficiency, etc. Note that improper use of specifications will only lead to wasted time during quality inspections (increasing the product cost) and frustration from the staff.

Boeing tested its prototype nose of the 777 by checking the performance of "Catia-man," a computer-generated human model. The prototype was built to confirm that airline crews could be as agile in the 777 nose as "Catia-man" (Norris, 1995).

Boeing devised a giant laboratory that contained every system used on the aircraft. The $370 million Integrated Aircraft Systems

Laboratory linked engineering versions of every 777 systems in real time, allowing full "flights" to be enacted on the ground. Up to 57 major aircraft systems, 3500 line replaceable units and 20,000 parts were tested and integrated with other parts. Once the main aircraft systems were successfully "talking" to each other in the lab, testing moved to the three big integration labs. One lab tested avionics with real-time simulations of the aircraft in flight. A second lab validated the fly-by-wire flight control system. The third test lab simulated the cockpit. With completion of every test in the project, the prototype 777 was cleared for flight test in record time. The test program was designed to facilitate certification for 180-minute extended-range twin operations (ETOPS). This extended service allowed airlines to fly routes that involved long flights across water, three hours (180 minutes) away from the nearest airport. After passing a series of rigorous tests during the year following the first test flight on June 12, 1994, the FAA approved, on May 30, 1995, the 180-minute ETOPS for the Boeing 777.

5.2.7 Send to Production

If testing proves that the product is of acceptable quality, then the product can enter the production phase. Thoughts of the production phase likely begin during the detailed design stage. As engineers become more experienced, they will consider not only the design of the pieces of a product but also how the pieces will be made. While this background thought process occurs, it should not be allowed to narrow the mind of the designer. However, given two equal possibilities for product construction, the one that is proven or easier to manufacture might be the best alternative. Developing some idea of how a product should be manufactured can only help to speed up the design process. If the design engineer does not know how to manufacture a piece, the manufacturing engineers will help conceive of a manufacturing process.

During the early production phases, engineers decide exactly how each part should be made, what equipment it will require to make the parts, how fast the parts can be made, and what it takes to make the part. If there is no current way to make a part as specified, a method will be devised or the part may need to be redesigned. Also, during this phase, engineers will decide how they will ensure that the parts and the final product will meet quality standards or how they will meet the design specifications.

Once processes for manufacture of the product have been determined, production will begin. During early production, problems will arise and need to be addressed either by the manufacturing staff or the design staff, depending on the problem. With time and work, production will (ideally) become smoother and efficiency will improve.

The first commercial flight of Boeing 777 from London to Washington D.C. on June 7, 1995, was successful and trouble-free. The increased-gross-weight, longer-range 777-200 was first delivered in February 1997. This model was capable of flying the same number of passengers up to 8,860 miles. Boeing also developed a stretched version of the 777, providing three-class seating for 368 to 386 passengers on routes up to 6,720 miles. This high-capacity 777-300 enters service with launch customers Cathay Pacific Airways of Hong Kong. By June 2002, Boeing had an order for 600 Boeing-777s and more than 400 in service around the world, each costing between $137 to $185 million.

Boeing might not receive a reasonable rate of return for the capital spent on the building of the 777. However, a major payoff was applying the lessons learned from the 777 program to the production of the 737 – Boeing's longest running and most successful transport program (Brown, et al., 1997). The core of the wing, the shape of the chord for the 737, had been changed to apply the advanced aerodynamics of the 777 wing for improved performance at cruise speeds. Another feature of the 737-600/-700/-800 models is maintaining crew commonality with the flight deck of over 1,800 current generation 737s that have already been ordered. Even though Boeing recognized that the markets served by the different kinds of aircraft are different, its design methodology for Boeing-777 was effective in reducing unnecessary inventory and redesign of aircraft. The Boeing 777 received the 2002 Airline Technology Achievement Award from Air Transport World Magazine for pioneering improvements in the development process.

5.3 RISK

Risk is defined as "the severity of the consequences of an accident times the probability of its occurrence" (Bahr 202). This definition demonstrates two ways to reduce risks: either minimize the consequences or minimize the probability of occurrence. This equation appears simple enough to use, but upon further evaluation, we often know little about the two components of the equation.

First and foremost, when trying to establish the risk involved with the use or existence of a product, you must think negatively and try to establish failures that could potentially occur. (This is a good place for brainstorming.) While this task is not uplifting, the result of the analysis justifies the mindset to achieve a safer product. You must be able to think in terms of how people may be injured or die, how the environment may suffer, or both. If you do not think in these terms and take the approach that everything will be fine (a violation of Murphy's Law), the potential for many accidents will exist. However, if you can train your mind to creatively envision what may go wrong, steps can be taken to avoid the occurrence of accidents. Take for example, the common doorstop. You might wonder how this could injure someone. In ordinary use, could someone get poked in the eye? Could someone sprain their ankle by stepping on it? Is it a fire hazard? How about when used improperly? Could a child swallow it? A dog? You must be creative at first. Some ideas are preposterous and with experience could be overlooked. However, experience should never restrict risk analysis to the point of ineffectiveness. This is why we try to be methodical.

Once a possibility of an accident is established, the severity of an accident or failure must be determined. How does the engineer determine how severe an accident can be? It is not simple and usually relies on historical data, personal bias, and guesswork. We attempt to establish the severity of an event by looking at historical figures. We will look at records of plane crashes, poisonings, explosions, or falls and try to determine, for example, in an accidental detonation of dynamite, how often someone dies. Simple enough, it seems. It is likely the person holding the dynamite dies. How about the others around? Making an accurate estimate is difficult but is possible with help from statisticians. So we check for insurance records or safety reports from blasting companies. Is it likely that such records exist? So we are back to trying to establish a number ourselves. Do I have personal reasons for believing blasting is improper and inflicts too much destruction for the product it produces? Can this affect the numbers I create? Hopefully not! While this is a topic for engineering ethics, the risk analysis you are compiling now may be someone's guide in the future, just as you searched for records. As you can observe, we are often left with a mixture of history and prediction of the future in severity analysis, especially in new or previously unconsidered areas. It is important to accurately estimate the severity and use conservative figure. The units for severity are consequence/event and some examples are deaths/plane crash or vision loss/eye poke with doorstop.

How often does a dog swallow a doorstop? Not very often, I suppose. Maybe you know a dog that eats doorstops. I might suggest that the frequency of this occurrence is once per year. You might suggest that this would occur once a week. Frequency is measured in units of accidents/time and, as demonstrated, can be as subjective as the severity estimation. In the case of plane crashes, data might exist that suggests how many crashes occur per flight time or per year. Sometimes information has never been compiled and must be estimated. Once again, it is important for engineers to quantify this accurately.

Once we have the numbers for severity and frequency, we can calculate the risk of an accident in terms of consequence/time. This information is a good place to start in analyzing what the most devastating accidents are. There are a couple of mainstream methods for attacking risk problems. One method is called Fault Tree Analysis (FTA). The other is Failure Modes and Effects Analysis (FMEA)

FTA uses a combination of Boolean algebra notation and flowchart diagrams to predict scenarios for failure. The system starts with a failure, such as wing failure during flight in an aircraft. Possible causes for the failure are backed out and placed on a chart (Figure 13)

Figure 13: Example Fault Tree

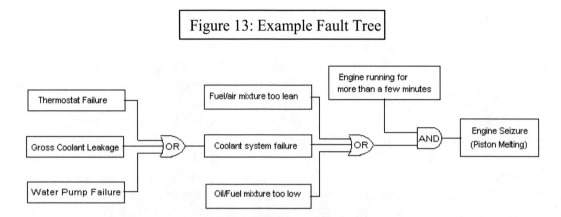

Fault Tree for Seizure of Water-Cooled Two-Stroke Engine
(Thompson, J.R. Engineering Safety Assessment An Introduction)

The causes for aircraft wing failure could be material related, environment related, or any number of other sources. Material related problems might arise from thermal issues, strength issues, or quality issues. Strength issues may include concepts such as yield strength and resonant vibration. Each of these has causes as well. In FTA, the goal is to reduce the scenarios back far enough to establish what the source of the problem is for each branch. Once the source is established, steps can be taken to reduce the likelihood that that branch will occur. The user of this tool might question how far back to trace the source of a problem. Is wing failure somehow related to the extinction of dinosaurs? Deciding where to stop will likely be determined by whoever is responsible for ensuring that this failure does not occur. For example, an aircraft manufacturer will take steps to ensure that the wing is properly assembled to the specifications required for safe operation. The aircraft manufacturer may also require steps be taken by their supplier of aluminum to ensure the proper level of purity and strength they expect from the material. This procedure will be repeated for different failures for the components of the end product. The trees are developed in conjunction with the numbers for risk to determine which trees could be most catastrophic.

Obviously, for something as complicated as an aircraft, this process could take time. Often, the failures that are deemed most catastrophic, such as the plane crashing, are attacked with the same urgency as high-risk failures. In the case of the aircraft, manufacturers have little choice but to do this process. Aside from the ethical matters, planes falling from the sky are bad for business. Airplane crashes usually result in multiple deaths instantaneously and cause greater public distress than deaths spread out over time. This puts more pressure on this industry to keep planes safe and reliable. Therefore, many engineers are typically employed by aircraft manufacturers to ensure a safe, but very expensive, product.

This brings into light the cost of safety and prevention of failure. Safety can be loosely defined as eliminating the risk of injury, death, or harm to the environment. A decision has to be made about how far the company should go to prevent accidents. In the aircraft example, the costs associated with safety are high but necessary. It is, however, passed on to the consumer in the form of higher ticket prices. The higher prices could make airline travel too expensive for some, eliminating potential demand for more aircraft. On the other hand, if the aircraft manufacturer did not take the time and invest the money in measures to identify and reduce risks, one might speculate that aircraft crashes might occur more frequently. More frequent crashes would likely result in less ticket purchases and, therefore, less aircraft purchases. While this is a broad generalization of how the cost of safety affects the company, it is a good basic demonstration.

The second effective tool in eliminating risks and improving quality and safety is Failure Modes and Effects Analysis (FMEA). The FMEA is an organized team approach that attempts to solve potential problems in a product as early as possible. The FMEA establishes failures in many areas such as product reliability, safety, customer satisfaction, manufacturing, and system performance. Some failures can be determined from historical data (including customer complaints) while others can be determined analytically (finite element modeling, for example). Once failures have been established, numbers can be assigned to the significance of the failure. The numbers are usually on a scale of 1 to 10, 10 being the worst. The numbers are assigned in the areas of severity and occurrence, as before, with the addition of a detection figure. Severity and occurrence have been previously discussed. Detection refers to the ability of the manufacturer to find a problem before it leaves the facility. This is a significant figure because information such as paint thickness, material properties, etc. are not easy to determine visually and require some detection device. This number might be 10 when trying to determine paint thickness by eye and could be reduced with a specialized measurement device. The numbers on the scale depend on the guidelines determined by the company. For severity, 1 injury in 100 might correspond to 10. For occurrence, 1 event in 1,000,000 might correspond to 1. Once these numbers are determined, they are multiplied together to create the Risk Priority Number (RPN). This number is used to prioritize corrective actions. Numbers above a certain RPN receive immediate attention.

In an FMEA, a failure with a high RPN might not be the only failure to receive immediate attention. Consider a failure that might cause certain death (Severity=10), but did not occur too frequently (Occurrence=2) and was easy to detect (Detection=1). This gives an RPN of 20, which is likely to be below the high priority level for the company. However, since the severity is so serious, steps will likely be taken immediately to reduce the occurrence to 1.

Several types of FMEAs are used in industry. Two of the most popular are design and manufacturing. The design FMEA will attempt to resolve as many design issues (potentially reliability, safety, ease of manufacture, etc.) as possible prior to manufacture, while the manufacturing FMEA will take steps to determine what can slow production of the product. The teams associated with each type (including types not mentioned here) are typically composed of people who are experts in that area. It makes little sense for the marketing department to be involved with the manufacturing FMEA but the department might be involved in the design FMEA. Of course, if the manufacturing FMEA team decides that a feature needs to be modified, the marketing department might need to approve the change because the change might impact the product's marketability. These two types of FMEAs overlap in scope and work together to ensure the best possible product reaches the customer.

The following news item shows that even though the design process was changed successfully during 1990-1994, subsequently, Boeing faced considerable risks in meeting its production deadlines during 1997-1999 (Business Week, 1998, 1999).

The Future of Engineering and Business Practices according to Phil Condit, CEO of Boeing Corporation (1998)

The shift from performance to value is new to aerospace, but not for other industries. It has happened to steel, appliances, and automobiles, and I could make that a much larger list. Each has felt the impact of value-based, customer-driven change. In fact, real costs are going down. I think the implications are pretty simple: we must change and change dramatically. We must change our industry, so we can provide value to our industry for the customer. The impact will be profound.

I believe engineering and business education will change dramatically too. Technology is changing rapidly. Back in medieval days, and even at the turn of the century, there was little change. Today, best estimates are we will have five fundamental changes in a lifetime. Education wants to specialize and divide subjects up into manageable pieces and focus on those pieces. But we need graduates with breadth.

I think business and engineering education needs to change. We need engineering graduates who understand economics. We need business graduates who understand technology. We need graduates who are willing to ask questions, "What does it really cost?" "How do you collaborate for a better product?" "How do you communicate new ideas effectively?" "How do you learn continuously?" These are four critical C's: cost, collaboration, communication, continuous learning. Let me talk about each one briefly.

First, *cost*. We need, for example, aerospace engineers who have a basic understanding about cost; who use cost data like weight data in the past. We need engineers who know how to design for manufacturing and for the reuse of system components. We need business people who understand how technology can be used to reduce cost. Business people who understand how to design for manufacturing and who know how to get good cost data rapidly to those who can affect cost.

Second, *collaboration*. Graduates must be able to work in inter-disciplinary teams. In the past, reward has been based on individual capability. You go through school getting grades for what you do. The same is usually true for a first job. You are chosen based on your capability. From that point on, you have to collaborate. I had an opportunity to teach a class of university students working in teams. Instead of individual grades, we decided to give a single grade to each team. One student raised his hand at the beginning and said that it wasn't fair, "What happens if I get a person on my team that doesn't pull all of their weight?" Welcome to how life really works.

A difficult thing about collaboration is "language" differences. Finance speaks one language. Another language is spoken on the shop floor; a structural engineer speaks another; and an electrical engineer yet another. Each has expertise. But I believe if the best product is to be designed and built, collaboration requires understanding each other. To collaborate effectively in teams, I believe, listening is critical. Especially to listen to what each team member is saying. The team also needs to be diverse. I think different backgrounds add to the richness of the team.

Third, *communication*. It's wonderful that individuals have great ideas and great concepts but if they can't communicate to other people, they will remain just that – concepts and ideas. People must be able to communicate their ideas and concepts, and that requires good verbal and writing skills. Communication also is two-way: you can't listen effectively when your mouth is open.

Finally, *continuous learning*. Technology is changing so rapidly, and tools are changing so quickly that to think we know today what we will need to know five years from now is preposterous. We need to learn "how to" effectively and efficiently learn, and it's an amazing challenge.
Cost. Collaboration. Communications. Continuous learning. They define, for me, what engineering and business education need to be about for the next century. We are in a world that is rapidly changing. If we are to be successful as companies, universities, governments, and individuals, we need to recognize the challenges and what that change means to all of us. I think that means cost,

Even though design changes were made at Boeing, the world's No.1 aerospace company has been beset by bad news for 1997. Cost overruns and production snafus contributed to a $178 million loss in 1997--the company's first in 50 years. And the economic crisis in Asia, a region responsible for one-third of Boeing's business, is slowing aircraft orders. The mounting labor tension stems from member anger about layoffs that are coming just as they finally managed to meet overly ambitious production goals. Boeing is set to crank out a record 620 planes in 1999. But it's still slashing payroll by 20%, from a peak of 238,000 last year, cuts that will hit the union's 48,000 members. The reason: a need to boost efficiency and bring down costs, coupled with an expected production downturn in 2000 because of a sharp falloff in orders from Asia.

5.4 SUMMARY

In this chapter you have seen the importance of effective engineering design in the real world. In the near future, you, the student, will be taking many courses that concentrate on the classroom applications of engineering theory such as sizing a shaft or determining its torsional characteristics. However, when considering whether or not to build a shaft out of titanium or aluminum, realize that in the workplace, aluminum may be the material of choice from a basic cost perspective, but the titanium may be necessary to prevent catastrophic failure (at increased cost).

You have also seen the design process graphically and through a simple example. You should be able to take this process and expand it to fit most of your engineering design projects. Remember that good design is an iterative process, and without iteration and careful consideration of design faults and consequences, the impact of failure can be immense.

SHORT ESSAY QUESTIONS

1) What are the major issues that you have to consider in engineering design?

2) Is design important in engineering jobs? Why?

3) Cost governs everything in design. Debate this point.

4) What factors affect the cost of a product?

5) Define risk.

6) How do you estimate risks in an engineering design?

7) Describe a fault tree analysis.

8) Describe a failure modes and effects analysis.

9) Relate an incident where you had to perform a design and what factors were important to you in performing this task.

STUDENT ASSIGNMENT

Individual Exercises

Pick a basic item in the room in which you are sitting (with a minimal amount of parts). List the parts and make notes of the design features that stand out as selling points (comfort, color, style, materials, etc.). Describe how you think these might increase the cost of a product (does the process appear precise, product difficult to assemble, product impossible to resist purchasing, etc.)

Team Exercises

1. Select a simple item in the room and brainstorm about the potential failures associated with it. Try to estimate figures for severity and frequency (occurrence) to achieve a total risk. Describe what could be done to reduce the risk.
2. Select another item and try to determine the critical considerations (measures to reduce risk) that might have been considered when designing the product.

REFERENCES

AT&T, *Design to Reduce Technical Risk,* McGraw-Hill, Inc., New York, NY, 1993.

Bahr, N.J., *System Safety Engineering and Risk Assessment: A Practical Approach.* Taylor and Francis, Washington, DC, 1997.

Bernstein, A., *Unions are Worried about Job Security -- the CEO's Deck,* Business Week, July 5, 1999.

Birmingham, R., Graham C., Robert D., and Maffin, D. *Understanding Engineering Design.* Prentice Hall Europe, Hemel Hempstead, England, 1997.

Brown, K., Ramanathan, K.V., Schmitt, T.G., and McKay, M., *"The Boeing Commercial Airplane Group: Design Process Evolution,"* 1997 *Decision Sciences Institute Conference*, p. 1341, Also available from *ECCH Publications*, 397-037-1.

Condit, P., *"Change and Challenge: Engineering the 21st Century,"* Chairman and Chief Executive Officer, Anderson Chandler Lecture Series, University of Kansas, School of Business, October 15, 1998. http://www.boeing.com/news/speeches/current/condit101598.html

Condit, P. M., *"Focusing on the Customer: How Boeing Does it,"* Research-Technology Management, 37(1): Jan/Feb. 1994, pp. 33-35.

Dym, C.L., *Engineering Design: A Synthesis of Views*, Cambridge University Press, Cambridge, UK, 1994.

Ertas, A. and Jones, J.C., *The Engineering Design Process*, John Wiley and Sons, Inc., New York, NY, 1996.

Hyman, B., *Fundamentals of Engineering Design.* Prentice Hall, Upper Saddle River, NJ, 1998.

National Research Council, *Improving Engineering Design.* National Academy Press, Washington, DC, 1991.

Norris, G., *"Boeing's Seventh Wonder,"* IEEE Spectrum, October 1995, pp. 20-23.

Petroski, H. *To Engineer is Human: the Role of Failure in Successful Design*, St. Martin's Press, New York, 1985.

Renihardt, A. and Browder, S., *Can a New Crew Buoy Boeing?,* Business Week, September 14, 1998.

Sabbagh, Karl, *Twenty First Century Jet, The Making and Marketing of the Boeing 777*, Scribner, New York: 1996.

Snyder, C., Snyder, C., and Sankar, C., *The Use of Information Technologies in the Process of Building the Boeing 777,* The Journal of Information Technology Management, Vol. IX, No. III, 1998, pp. 31-42

Stamatis, D.H., *Failure Modes and Effects Analysis.* ASQC Quality Press, Milwaukee, WI, 1995.

Starfield, A.M., Smith, K.A., and Bleloch, A.L. *How to Model it: Problem Solving for the Computer Age,* McGraw-Hill, New York, NY, 1990.

Stonecipher, H.C., "*Cost: The New Frontier in Aerospace Engineering,*" President and Chief Operating Officer, The Boeing Company, Address to Financial Executives Institute of Seattle, Jan. 28, 1999.
http://www.boeing.com/news/speeches/current/stonecipher012899.html
Weston, J. Fred, Scott Besley, and Eugene F. Brigham, *Essentials of Managerial Finance.* 11th ed. Dryden Press, Fort Worth, TX, 1996.

Woolsey, J.P., "*The Revolution Grows,*" *Air Transport World*, 33(12): Dec. 1996, pp. 51-56.

6 Basics of Operating Systems

LEARNING GOALS

- Identify the different operating systems used in computers
- Define the different terms associated with computers
- Differentiate between Windows NT and CE
- Identify the features of new operating systems that are available

6.1 INTRODUCTION

This chapter discusses the various, generic aspects of operating systems. For companies to have an accurate and dependable POS system, it is important to keep in mind the intricate steps that must occur within any system to accomplish elementary operations. The pictures below show the locations of the important elements that will be discussed further in this chapter.

Display and Input   Storage, Memory, Software, and Hardware

Figure 14: Operating system elements

6.2 INSTRUCTIONS FROM BITS AND BYTES

Bits are the smallest units of memory that are measured in computing terminology. Computers are designed to store data and execute instructions in groups of bits known as bytes. An instruction is a command given to a computer's processor by a program. These instructions are given in a sequence of 0's and 1's (delivered in the form of bytes) that describe an operation the computer is to perform. The processor, also known as the CPU or central processing unit, responds to these instructions and carries them outs in a one-at-a-time sequence. This one-at-a-time sequence is contained in a program that is held in the memory. For more information on **Bits**, **The Binary System**, **Bytes**, and **Measuring Memory**, please refer to **the CD-ROM.**

6.3 CENTRAL PROCESSOR UNITS

Invented by Intel in 1971, central processor units are chips that contain millions of transistors that are responsible for PC data processing. The CPU is considered to be the "brains" of a computer because it is central to the computer's operation; it either executes or controls all data transfer or processing. The processing of data is done by moving and calculating data that are given to it from memory. The CPU is constantly processing data with data coming from the memory, being processed and passed back to the memory in its resolved form to other units within the computer.

Below is a logical representation of this process:

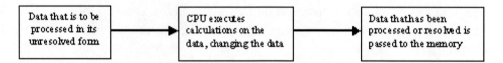

Figure 15: Data processing steps

The data is passed from the memory to the CPU via the system bus. The system bus is the wiring within a computer that sends or receives data to and from input/output devices, a computer's main memory and its CPU. The bus works in serial, with one bit traveling along the system bus one at a time. In the illustration above, the arrows represent the system bus.

The central processor receives two types of data for execution: (1) instructions and (2) data that are to be handled according to the instructions. For any operation that is occurring in a computer, these two data types must be present. For more information on Central Processor Units and Processor Chips, please refer to the CD-ROM.

The logical flow of these two types of data and the CPU are illustrated below:

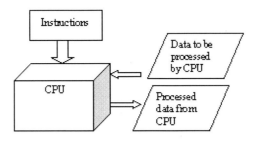

Figure 16: Central processor data flow

6.4 TYPES OF MEMORY

Data is generally kept in three main areas. These three areas are storage, RAM, and ROM. Within the types of memory (RAM and ROM), several variants of each type exist. Each of the types of memory is best suited for different situations and functions. For more information on **RAM**, **ROM**, and **PROM**, please refer to **the CD-ROM**. **EPROM** is discussed below.

6.4.1 EPROM

EPROM (Erasable Programmable Read-Only Memory) improves on PROM technologies. EPROM chips can be erased using specialized equipment after they've been removed from a computer. Once the chip is blank, a programmer is able to install new instructions.

Shining an intense ultraviolet light through a small window located on the memory chip will erase EPROM chips. The window on the chips is usually covered to block out light in order to protect the data that has been installed on an EPROM chip. Although ordinary room lighting does not contain enough ultraviolet light to cause erasure, bright sunlight can cause a full or partial erasure. For this reason EPROM chips are usually covered with a label when not installed in the computer, making them easily recognizable. For information on **The History of EPROM,** please see **the CD-ROM.**

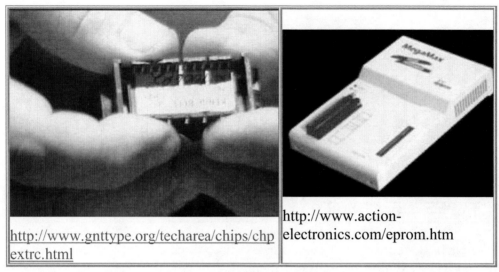

Figure 17: EPROM Chips

6.5 VERSION 2000 SYSTEMS

The Version 2000 POS required a fixed keyboard for the input of data. EPROM memory was favored in this situation because the meaning of the input to the POS system could be changed to reflect changes in the menu offered by the company. In this sense, the EPROM technologies offered a limited degree of flexibility to the corporate management.

Available space on the keyboard for order entry can quickly become an issue for the corporate management. To alleviate this problem, the input keyboard made use of a "shift" key to allow a single key to represent more than one function. When a button is pressed on the keyboard, the data sent to CPU from the EPROM's memory area contained additional data describing if the input was accompanied by "shift key" input. The use of the shift key method for order entry allows the POS to continue using the Version 2000 systems with an expanding menu offering and an aging technology.

6.6 OPERATING SYSTEMS

Operating systems (often abbreviated as "OS") are programs that, after being initially loaded into a computer, manage all the other programs in a computer. To use an operating system in a computer, it must be first loaded into the RAM from the storage; this process is known as "booting" a computer (the name derives from a strap that was common on boots. These "bootstraps" allowed a boot to be pulled on over the foot). The

140

BIOS program (see previous example) manages the loading process of the operating system. For more information on the Boot-Up Process, Loading verses installing an Operating System, Applications, Tasking, Interfacing with the Operating System, and Common Functions of Operating Systems, please refer to the CD-ROM. GUI and Windowing Systems are discussed below.

6.6.1 Graphical User Interface (GUI)

The most popular method for interacting with an OS and most application programs is through the use of a graphical user interface (or GUI, pronounced GOO-ee). The use of a GUI method for interaction with the OS typically makes use of a mouse to make the use and navigation of an operating system easier to users. GUI interfaces make use of graphical icons that represent certain tasks available to users, eliminating the need to remember commands. Apple used the concept of a GUI in their first Macintosh computers. Soon after, Microsoft used many of the same ideas in their first version of the Windows operating system for IBM-compatible PCs.

For example, to run a program from storage using text-based commands a user would have to type the program name that it was trying to run followed by .exe. A GUI interface allows a user to use a mouse to "click" on an icon to run the program (the icon executes the application name with the .exe command for the user).

GUI interfaces give a degree of intuitiveness to a computer. By depicting tasks in easily recognizable icons, a user can infer with a higher degree of accuracy what will occur when input is given. For example, the EPROM POS systems used by the company did not have a GUI interface for the sales associates ringing up orders. Since this computer lacks a GUI, it is reasonable to expect a higher percentage of incorrect inputs while attempting to ring up an order. To alleviate this problem, a touch screen depicting icons of the items on the menu would increase the degree of order accuracy by a sales associate.

GUI often uses metaphors for familiar objects in real life to aid the user. This includes items such as a desktop, a view through a window, or even sounds depicting actions (like a sound of sizzling for the selection "bacon" on a POS system). Common elements of a GUI interface include such things as: drop-down menus, pop-up menus, graphical buttons, scrolling bars along edges, use of a mouse, icons representing tasks, and, with increasing use of multimedia, sounds.

6.6.2 Windowing Systems

A windowing system works within a GUI interface environment to make use of a computer's graphical display presentation resources among multiple application programs at the same time. Often users have a number of separate application programs running at the same time (see multitasking above). The use of separate windows for each application allows a user to interact with each application program and to quickly bound between applications without the need to reinitiate each application program. Multitasking and the use of a windowing system allow a user to have different application programs occurring in the GUI environment in order to increase productivity by the user.

Graphical representation of a GUI interface

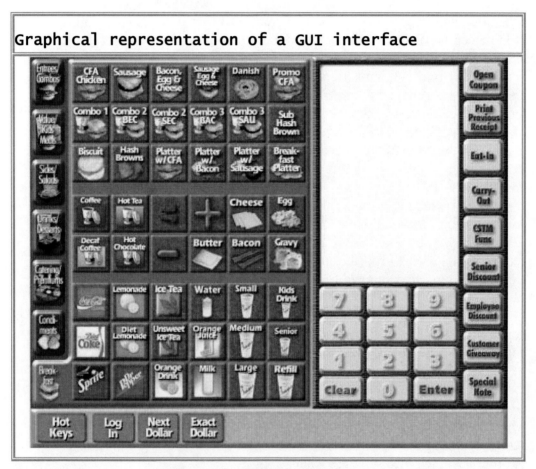

Figure 18: GUI Interface

6.7 COMMONLY USED OPERATING SYSTEMS

UNIX (used in SUN workstations), Microsoft's Windows family (Windows 95, Windows 98, Windows NT, Windows CE), IBM's OS/2, Apple's OS X [ten], and Linux are all examples of operating systems. There are many more operating systems available depending on the computer system that is purchased from a vendor. Frequently, a computer vendor will specify the operating systems that will work well with the hardware. The MIS personnel have to make the choice between the hardware and operating system combinations. This decision is critical since operating systems are available for purchase in most computer software stores. It is common to purchase operating systems in the form of CD-ROMs or floppy disks (3.5-inch magnetic diskettes), although they can also be downloaded from the World Wide Web. Some operating systems are also free (such as Linux) and can be retrieved though the methods listed above.

Packaging for various operating systems for consumer purchase. From left to right these operating systems are Windows NT Workstation, OS/2, and Windows NT Server.

Packaging for the Windows CE operating system development kit. This kit is used to customize Windows CE applications for individual consumers.

Figure 19: Operating system software packaging

6.7.1 DOS

DOS (for Disk Operating System) is a non-GUI; line-by-line oriented command-driven operating system, lacking a "friendly" user interface. Its prompt to enter a command looks like this:

C:\>

Where the "C" command stood for the local hard drive (the hard drive used by that computer). The other elements were prompts for the user. For example, to run the word processing application program called "basic" in the DOS operating system, the user would type "basic.exe" and the application runs. At this point the operating system would manage the application and the computer's resources like all other operating systems.

Figure 20: Packaging of the DOS operating system for consumer purchase in 1981

DOS Features

DOS was the first widely installed operating system used in personal computers. Indeed, the first personal computer developed for IBM on August 12th, 1981 by Bill Gates and the Microsoft Corporation used DOS.

Later in 1985, the first Microsoft Windows operating system using a GUI interface would become available for consumer purchase for $99. This first version of Windows would really be an application program that ran "on top" of the MS-DOS operating system. Today, the Windows operating systems available continue to support DOS for special purposes.

6.7.2 Windows CE

The "thin" option POS given to the company used Microsoft's Windows CE (abbreviated as WinCE) for the operating system software. WinCE has the ability to multitask and is a fully preemptive OS environment that supports up to eight levels of priority. Windows CE is considered by Microsoft to be the "light" version of the Windows 9X series. The user interface makes use of a GUI environment and uses the familiar Windows interface common in personal computers. The "CE" is reported to have originally stood for "Consumer Electronics", however Microsoft declines to comment what CE stands for.

WinCE is targeted specifically toward hardware with limited resources. It is commonly found in handheld devices such as palm-sized computers (often known as Personal Digital Assistants or PDA's) and other space-constrained devices. The CE operating system is making more appearances in an embedded form for such devices as microwaves, gas station pumps, and information kiosks. The modular design of Windows CE OS enables embedded-systems developers and application developers to customize it for a variety of products such as POS systems. This design of the OS minimizes the memory footprint required for application program operations. The "thin" option for the company was to use a custom installation of Windows CE embedded into a type of ROM memory card. Additionally, the customized and focused design of WinCE allows for abbreviated system boot-ups making it useful for time-constrained operations.

Windows CE Features

Windows CE allows embedded-computer system developers to leverage their existing Windows-based programming skills for development. In addition to the ability to multitask, Windows CE supports many common APIs and several additional programming interfaces to help manage application programs through the CE operating system. WinCE directly supports many kinds of hardware peripherals and devices, such as keyboards, mouse devices, touch panels, serial ports, Ethernet, modems, USB devices, audio devices, parallel ports, printer devices, and storage devices. Windows CE also provides storage and retrieval of database records. Other than a custom installing Windows CE on a terminal head in a POS system, the only other install requirements for a POS system are the necessary device drivers.

Very much similar to networked computer, a thin POS device may make use of a server for data storage; typically a Windows CE POS terminal head can only hold a day or so worth of orders independently of the server. In this sense, the devices are truly thin clients- applications appear to be running on the client but are actually running on the server. This configuration allows for the system to be free of hard drives or floppy drives for boot up and data storage. Also, CPU requirements can be kept to a minimum by placing any needed application programs onto a server.

Another feature of Windows CE is its ability to make use of the Windows 32-bit architecture. The result of this is that important software functions that may be needed (such as the acceptance of credit cards at the POS) could be written for the device much more easily and much more cost effectively than would be possible with a proprietary architecture.

Windows CE also allows for communications with a wide range of applications. WinCE features a fully functioning TCP/IP capability, eliminating much of the time and costs associated with developing a proprietary communications protocol. Having this capability could essentially make each POS terminal head a node on a network for the company. A corporate wide area network (WAN) within the organization could be conceivable. Store operators could address software and other store management problems by accessing the WAN for help. This could serve to increase centralized company control at the corporate headquarters. Also, data mining techniques at the corporate headquarters could be used to realize trends in data much sooner and in greater detail than is possible with non-networked POS devices. The built in communications abilities would also allow for easily communicating with the Internet in the future.

Finding Windows CE Programmers

With more than 5 million Windows 32-bit system developers worldwide, there are many experienced programmers who already know how to develop for the Microsoft Windows CE platform. This serves to lower training costs and shortens system development time. Developers for a thin POS solution would not be forced to learn a closed proprietary system- closed proprietary systems tend to repel developer talent in an industry as it limits their marketable skill sets.

Platform Builder is a set of tools and pre-configured APIs that enables a developer to program custom embedded computer system applications that use Windows CE. Platform Builder is designed with the goal of creating a familiar and easy-to-use development environment for the system developer.

6.7.3 Windows NT

Windows NT Features

Windows NT comes in two forms: Windows NT Server and Windows NT Workstation. The company was only considering Windows NT Workstation for its POS terminals OS. Windows NT (from here on only Windows NT Workstation will be discussed) was
designed to be an OS for those needing advanced capability over other Windows OS products. It was considered to be a faster performing and more fail-safe environment than Windows 95 or Windows 98 (Microsoft claims that this speed was up to 20% faster for 32-bit applications).

Windows NT also featured many more security and management functions that were not available with other Windows operating systems such as Windows CE. Windows NT would require that each POS terminal head have its own database with its own applications resident on each device. The network would really only be required for the synchronizing of data for transmission back to corporate headquarters. The elimination of network dependence adds a layer of independence to protect against data loss in the event that the network became unavailable. Since the data would be resident on each machine, backing up data without the network would be an available option to the storeowner.

Windows NT was considered to highly scalable because its use is so commonly used to meet business needs. This adds a degree of flexibility for the future that cannot be accurately predicted in specific industries such as the quick-service restaurant industry.

Windows NT has all of the abilities of the CE solution in terms of communications. It had the extended ability to run several other network protocols other than TCP/IP for ease of integration with other networks. These protocols include IP, IPX, DLC, and NetBEUI.

Windows NT also had similar graphical abilities that are featured in Windows CE.

Window NT had some advantages over the CE version. It was better supported with business applications and was widely used in several industries. Support was common, easily affordable, and there was a large labor force readily available. Developers for the Windows NT were also readily available and could be found affordably.

However, Windows NT was considered to have a larger footprint than Windows CE when in direct comparison. Windows NT would also require that the terminal head have moving parts for operation. Window CE allows use of other business applications, like Word Processing, Financial/Accounting, Graphic Design, on the POS Compatible for Internet and e-mail access.

Finding Windows NT Programmers

Microsoft actively promotes the widespread availability of application developers for the Windows NT environment as part of its marketing campaign to promote the operating system. Windows NT also enjoys widespread use in a variety of industries ensuring that a work force will available for application development when needed.

Microsoft goes a step further by offering certification programs that relate to the Windows NT operating system. A certification tract, known as Microsoft Certified Systems Engineer or MCSE, is highly recognized in technology related disciplines for networking computers running Windows NT as the operating system. Microsoft allows offers other courses and certifications ranging from application development to effective management of the security features.

6.7.4 Summary of Operating Systems

Having discussed the different operating systems, the two operating systems, CE and NT could be compared as shown in Table 3.

Table 3: Windows CE vs. Windows NT

Feature	Windows CE	Windows NT Embedded
Operating System Version	3.0	4.0 service pack 5

147

	x86, Mips, SH3, SH4, StrongARM, ARM, Power PC, Strong ARM, Hitatchi	x86 (Pentium, AMD K5/6, Cyrix 5x86/6x86), Mips, Power PC
Supported CPUs	x86, Mips, SH3, SH4, StrongARM, ARM, Power PC, Strong ARM, Hitatchi	x86 (Pentium, AMD K5/6, Cyrix 5x86/6x86), Mips, Power PC
CPU Speed	Runs on as little as 80 mhz, can operate at 500+ mhz	Recommended 300 mhz, can operate at 500+ mhz
Multiprocessor	None - uniprocessor	Up to 32, server edition, 4 workstation edition
Multitasking	Preemptive - limited to 32 applications, supports threads	Preemptive, supports threads
Memory - minimum	1 MB execution, no storage required	12 MB execution, 8 MB storage w/o networking, 16 Mb execution, 16 MB storage w/networking

Feature	Windows CE	Windows NT Embedded
Paging	Dynamic paging based on available internal ram	Paging file to secondary storage (fixed or dynamic) or disable paging
Utilities	Command Shell, Pocket Internet Explorer (equivalent to Internet Explorer 4.0), Pocket Inbox, Help Engine - Client Functionality, Windows Terminal Server Client	Command shell, text editing, Windows Explorer, Microsoft Management Console, network configuration utilities, Windows help engine, task scheduling, and others - Server or Workstation functionality
General Features	Headless support Diskless support - Boot from flash media, or CD Rom (Sega Dreamcast boots from CD)	Headless support Diskless support - Boot from flash media or CD Rom
Security	None	NTFS, application level
Display	Optimized for smaller displays, supports up to 800 x 600	640 x 480 and larger standard displays

148

Communications Protocols	TCP/IP, PPP, SLIP, PAP, CHAP, HTTP, IrDA	TCP/IP, IPX/SPX, AppleTalk, NetBEUI, PPP, SLIP, CSLIP, PAP, CHAP, PPTP, HTTP, RPC, SNMP

Feature	Windows CE	Windows NT Embedded
Data Storage	ATA Flash, Linear Flash, PC Card hard disk, CompactFlash hard disk, IDE hard disk - FAT format - no capacity limit, CD-ROM	ATA Flash, M-Systems Disk on a Chip- Max capacity is 144 MB flash, Bootable CD-ROM
Data Storage Formats	FAT, FAT32	FAT, NTFS, compression
Power/CPU Management	Power management for extended battery life, instant on capable	Same as Windows CE
API	Subset of Win32	Full Win32
Development Tools	Platform Builder ($999, not disclosed per license pricing) Requires Visual C++	Target Designer ($395). Target Designer + RTX ($1,950 plus $395 per license)

6.8 CONCLUSION

This chapter has dealt with the operating systems used in computers. We first discovered how instructions in the form of bytes are given to the central processing unit. The central processing unit stores and retrieves data and instructions. Data is generally kept in storage, RAM, and ROM. An advanced form of ROM is EPROM. EPROM Systems offer flexibility in the form of EPROM chips. The Version 2000 POS Systems favor the use of EPROM. Operating Systems are programs that manage all other programs in the computer system. Interaction with the operating system is often made through the use of graphical user interfaces (GUI). In order to determine which operating system is best for a company, the fundamentals of computer systems must be understood so that the advantages of each operating system may be analyzed according to what a company desires for its POS Systems.

SHORT ESSAY QUESTIONS

1. What is the smallest unit of memory and what is a group of 8 of them called?
2. What is the job of the CPU?
3. What company invented the first CPU and in what year?
4. Describe the processing of data done by the CPU.
5. Name 2 types of data the central processor receives for execution.
6. What three main areas is data kept?
7. What is the difference in PROM and EPROM chips?
8. Why was the shift key invented?
9. What is the function of the operating system? Name 3 commonly used operating systems.
10. What does bootstrap mean?
11. What is the most popular method for interacting with an operating system? Describe this method.
12. Name a few real-life metaphors associated with the Windows GUI.
13. Name 2 software and hardware components.
14. What does DOS stand for and how does it differ from Windows?
15. What was the first widely installed operating system?

KEY WORDS

API
BIOS
Bits
Bootstraps
Bytes
Central processing unit (CPU)
DOS
EPROM
Friendly user interface
Graphical User Interface (GUI)
Hardware
Hardware peripherals
Instruction
Operating system
Personal digital assistant (PDA)
Platform Builder
Point-of-Sales (POS)
Processor
Random access memory (RAM)
Read-only memory (ROM)
Robustness
Software
Storage
TCP/IP
Thin option
Wide area network (WAN)
Windowing System
Windows CE
Windows NT

REFERENCES

http://www.action-electronics.com/eprom.htm

http://www.gnttype.org/techarea/chips/chpextrc.html

7 Scientific Decision Making

LEARNING GOALS

- Differentiate between prescriptive and descriptive methods in solving real-world engineering problems
- Explain what decision support methods are available to help engineers perform their jobs
- List the categories of computer-aided systems available to help you make decisions
- Explain and use Decision Trees
- Explain and use *Expert Choice*, a Decision Support System
- Describe the psychological considerations involved in decision-making
- Give examples of the type of decisions engineers must make to fulfill their job responsibilities

7.1 INTRODUCTION

The essence of ultimate decision remains impenetrable to the observer - often, indeed to the decider himself.... There will always be the dark and tangled stretches in the decision making process - mysterious even to those who may be more intimately involved. - John F. Kennedy (from Sorensen, 1963).

For a product to achieve its full potential, it must be manufactured at the lowest cost possible, within a scheduled time, with low risk for the company and the customer, and in an ethical manner. Engineers are in charge of designing and manufacturing the product within budget and time constraints. As they perform these tasks, engineers must make important technical decisions on many occasions throughout their careers. Engineers make these decisions even though they may not have complete information about the market and product specifications. Aside from technical factors, engineers must often consider cost factors, scheduling pressures, risk levels, management criteria, and ethical dilemmas before making a technical decision.

Engineering decisions are frequently based on a deterministic analysis that applies principles from physics, chemistry, or mathematics. For example, engineers consider the load and stress factors when designing cantilevers, beams, and support structures for a bridge.

However, as the bridge is being built, engineers may not have considered other factors such as budget changes, varied skills of employees, changes to the order by customers, the possibility of severe weather patterns, and so on. Considering these factors requires the engineers to use probabilistic analysis in making their designs. Nowadays, the use of probabilistic analysis with reliability-based safety factors is well accepted in the engineering profession (Ang and Tang, 1975). The discipline of decision science has evolved and matured so that it is now in a position to help engineers include uncertainties in their models, thereby encouraging the best possible decisions given probabilistic estimates.

This chapter shows how decision support methods are used in solving real-world engineering problems. It also describes various decision support methods that are available to help engineers perform their jobs. A few of these methods are described in detail. We expect that by understanding the principles provided in this chapter, you will be able to design and develop innovative new products and processes that will help society. We also expect that by learning these methods you will further hone your decision-making skills, enhancing your ability to be successful in your future career.

7.2 IMPORTANCE OF DECISION-MAKING

An engineer/manager routinely makes decisions that have a strong impact on the quality and type of products that are produced by a company. Many people will use these products and the consequences of bad design decisions have to borne by those who invented, designed, manufactured, marketed, and sold poor products to society. The examples shown in Appendices 1 and 2 illustrate the consequences resulting from decisions made by engineers.

Appendix 1 illustrates practical examples of how a prototype optimization model was used to budget, plan, and manage prototype test fleets, reducing annual prototype costs by more than $250 million. The box also discusses the optimization models that evaluate current and future maintenance needs of bridges. These examples show that innovative designs based on good decision-making by engineers are the key to successful companies.

Appendix 2 discusses what went wrong at Shiva Corporation, a once attractive company that produced routers and other telecommunications equipment for the Virtual Private Network market. At one point during 1996, its stock was selling for over $87 per share and it was considered a strong competitor in remote access products; *PC Magazine* endorsed its products for many years. However, as time went on, the products of the company failed to sell well and it was not able to compete successfully against the bigger companies in the same field. Revenues decreased and the price of the stock sank to $2.75 per share during 1998. This led to Shiva's eventual demise and merger with the Intel Corporation, yielding $6 per share to Shiva shareholders in 1999. This example shows that even though their engineers were able to design and produce award-winning products, a company may not survive if its management team is not able to convert the innovations into products that sell.

7.3 DEFINITIONS

Decision-making is defined as intentional and reflective choice in response to a problem. This ability is the fundamental characteristic that distinguishes humans from lower forms of life (Kleindorfer, et al., 1993).

Decision-making is the process of selecting a course of action from among all choices available to the decision-maker in order to solve a specific problem or set of problems (Badawy, 1995).

7.4 TYPES OF DECISION-MAKING PROCESSES

The discipline of decision science has been created to understand and improve the decision making abilities of individuals, groups, and organizations (Kleindorfer, et al., 1993). According to this discipline, there are two major categories of decision-making processes: prescriptive and descriptive. Prescriptive analysis indicates how decisions should be made according to a set of well-defined criteria. These are the kinds of directions that you as a student are used to receiving from your teachers, and parents. Examples are when your mom asks, "Did you brush your teeth tonight?" or when your instructor states, "The essay test will include material from Chapters 2 and 3." Prescriptive decision-making theory provides a decision-maker with pre-specified alternatives, consequences, states-of-the-world, preferences, and beliefs. It addresses the question, "Given what has happened in the past, what should I do next?" rather than, "Why did it happen?" or "Why did somebody do it?" (Bell, Raiffa, and Tversky, 1988). In contrast, descriptive analysis describes how people actually make decisions. You may not brush your teeth at night until after you visit the dentist. When the dentist stresses the need to brush your teeth regularly, then you might make the conscious decision to brush your teeth every night. As you may be aware, the process by which each person makes decisions varies significantly. Some people are very predictable in the decisions they make given certain information; others are not that predictable, even though the situation might seem similar. Descriptive decision-making theories deal with the question, "Why did it happen?" "Why did somebody do it?" "How would I deal with it?" (Bell, Raiffa, and Tversky, 1988).

The case study methodology combines prescriptive and descriptive decision-making theories. The materials in many textbooks are prescriptive; they tell you what to do in a particular situation. Your instructors test you on whether you were able to retain the specific domain knowledge provided in the books. Some of you may find this process tedious since you may not always understand why these theories are important and how they will be useful to you later in your career.

In contrast, case studies describing real-world situations are descriptive. They describe what happened in a plant at a particular time, provide a set of related facts, and ask you to make a decision. When you work on the exercises associated with the case studies, you will have an opportunity to apply the prescriptive theories you have already learned to solve the descriptive problems presented in the case studies. However, bear in mind that the engineers and managers presented in the case studies may not have had the time or the resources to apply these theories in practice. We hope that as you go on to take other courses in engineering that are difficult and challenging, you will continuously ask yourself, "how can this theory be used to improve a product or process?" Your future employers definitely expect you to have learned the latest engineering tools and techniques in your curriculum. The challenge for you is whether you can apply the knowledge you gained in school to solving real-world problems. That is where the skills you learn working on the case studies will be of most use to you.

7.4.1 Prescriptive Models for Decision-Making

The prescriptive models for decision-making are based on the assumption that human beings are rational beings trying to achieve the best result given constraints. Figure 21 shows a flow chart for the decision-making process that is based on the models mentioned in Kleindorfer, et al. (1993), Badawy (1995) and Clemen (1996). Each step in the flowchart is explained below.

Understand the Situation and Identify the Objectives
The first step in making a good decision is to understand the situation where the problem has occurred. Once you understand the company's background and the industry information given in each case study, you can identify the objectives to be achieved. The objective should be practical, operational, and attainable. The statement of an objective should also include explicit references to any constraints that may affect the decision. It is critical to understand the objectives before proceeding to the next step.

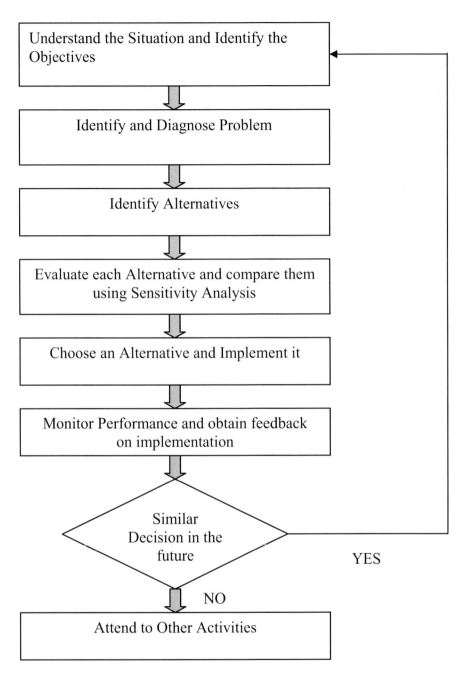

Figure 21: Decision-Making Flowchart

Identify and Diagnose the Problem

The second step in the decision-making process is to recognize the problem and analyze it. A good engineer must have the ability to design products that meet the needs of his or her company's customers. A customer will buy a product if it solves an existing problem and gives greater satisfaction than alternative uses for the money. The engineer's design is best assessed in relation to money, markets, and competition. In a business environment, the engineer's employer is concerned with the profit contribution that would be obtained by satisfying a market. It is the consequence of design, not the nature of design, which is the employer's primary concern (Twiss, 1998).

In order to identify and diagnose the problem correctly, you must gather information regarding facts, assumptions, and stakeholders' values. A stakeholder is anyone who has a major stake in the decision being made. This includes a company's customers, employees, shareholders, suppliers, and so on.

You must ask yourself questions in order to identify the problem. What is the real problem? How is this problem related to the goals, values, and needs of the organization? Who are the primary and secondary stakeholders? How well do you understand their goals, views, objectives, constraints, and agendas? The net outcome of this step is accurate problem identification.

Identify Alternatives

A careful examination and analysis of the objectives and problem statement can often reveal alternatives that were not obvious at the outset. Research and creativity can play a strong role in identifying alternatives that may not be apparent to a person well entrenched in the problem situation. Group participation, brainstorming sessions, and an environment that encourages unusual ideas are important in identifying the widest possible range of alternatives. Barriers to identifying good alternatives include: (a) limiting proposals to those areas that you control or are knowledgeable about; (b) proposing only solutions that have been used in similar occasions in the past; and (c) creating solutions that solve the immediate problem but do not deal with long-term impacts.

Evaluate Alternatives and Compare them Using Sensitivity Analysis

The fourth step is to evaluate each choice. Comparing alternatives requires the development of criteria or yardsticks to judge the value of each alternative. The criteria have to be identified based on the objectives and the environment in which the decision solution will be implemented. You need to evaluate each alternative with respect to the criteria and arrive at a decision. The process of arriving at a decision requires a combination of objective facts and intuition.

157

Computer-aided decision support systems (DSS) and statistical tools are available that can assist you in this step. These software packages answer "what-if" questions such as "If I make a slight change in one or more aspects of this model, does the decision change?" As an example, the commonly used software Turbotax™ has integrated "what-if" capabilities. After you graduate, you will have to file tax returns (some of you might already have to do this). An important question faced by married tax-filers is: should I file as "married filing jointly" or "married filing separately"? You might pay less tax depending on which you choose. To help an individual make this decision, Turbotax™ has a built-in "What-If Worksheet" that provides an option where you can perform a sensitivity analysis on whether to file jointly or separately. The software computes the results of tax due for each alternative. In the worksheet, you can experiment by computing the taxes on both incomes versus reporting them individually. In some years, it might be advantageous for you to file jointly and in other years separately. In addition, you might be able to devise strategies to reduce taxes in the future by changing the ownership of your Certificates of Deposit or stocks to your spouse or children. Decision support system tools also provide you with the ability to evaluate the sensitivity of changing some of the assumptions or allocations among the alternatives. These analyses may change your perception of the problem, preferences, and possibilities. Performing sensitivity analysis calculations is an important and critical part of the decision-making process.

Choose the Best Alternative and Implement It

The fifth step is to choose the alternative that best solves the problem based on the constraints. Most people modify the solutions that the decision science model provides. Frequently, people *satisfice*; in other words, they search, find a few alternatives, and choose the one that satisfies them for the present (Simon, 1957).

Satisfice: Individuals do not look for the best or optimal decision in most instances. They search for alternatives, stop at a reasonable alternative, and choose it. A theoretical model might predict that the person should have performed a lot more searches and chosen an optimal decision. These models do not normally include the time and effort involved in identifying and analyzing alternatives.

Even if your choice is accepted, it is important for your organization to buy in to your recommendation and implement it wholeheartedly. If you include those who will be affected by the decision in the process, the implementation is likely to be smoother. You also need to recognize that this decision is yours to champion. You have to stay focused, champion it and implement it. You must be confident in your decision and convincingly communicate your solution to the stakeholders. It is critical that you have faith in your choice. Others might question your choice and if you are not assertive in defending it, your choice might be rejected and a less effective substitute might be implemented. In large organizations, the implementation of your decision may be performed by different sets of individuals and if you do not communicate your intentions well enough, it is possible that the implementation might be very different from what you originally intended.

Monitor Performance and Obtain Feedback on Implementation

It is important for the organization to collect data on how well the decision was implemented and whether it solved the original problem. Instant feedback might be possible for simple decisions, but it might take years to evaluate complex decisions regarding research and development. Many organizations implement control processes to monitor performance and obtain feedback. As an engineer, you will be working with many different measurement devices and systems (flow meters, gauges, and so on). In addition, you will be working with software systems that monitor the flow of capital, funds, people, and other resources in the organization. It is important for you to obtain feedback from the different systems available so that you can continually improve your decisions.

Impact of the Decision-Making Process on Future Decisions

If your organization is able to monitor the performance of earlier decisions, a history log could be established that identifies the good and bad decisions made in the past. This could be used effectively in improving the decision-making process when similar problems occur in the future. Knowledge Management software packages help organizations track and improve their decision-making process. You should be aware, however, that although these tools and processes are valuable guides, they cannot guarantee good decisions. Employees, engineers, managers, and executives are still responsible for making the best choices by choosing, implementing, and monitoring the decisions.

7.5 COMPUTER-AIDED DECISION SUPPORT SYSTEMS TOOLS

Several computer-aided software systems are available to assist in decision-making. In this section, we will describe a number of them. By knowing something about each software system, you will be able to choose the most appropriate software for a given decision-making situation.

- *Decision Tree Software*: This software is helpful when making a decision under conditions of risk, such as whether to choose the cheapest design or the most expensive design. A Decision Tree is usually represented as a tree on its side with branches and subbranches. The branches generally represent alternatives that depend on the occurrence or nonoccurrence of probabilistic events. For example, Decision Trees are used to ensure that schedule, cost, and quality goals are met for large-scale refinery construction projects (Dey, 2002).

- *Linear and Integer Programming Software*: This software is helpful when allocating funds to develop a mix of products given capacity constraints, set-up costs, and production costs. The linear and integer programming method involves maximizing or minimizing an objective function subject to constraints, generally in the form of inequalities such as "greater than" or "less than." Sensitivity analysis allows you to change the parameters and see how it impacts the results. For example, the Stillwater Mining Company needed a tool for analyzing development and production scenarios in a new area of an underground platinum and palladium mine in Stillwater, Montana. They developed a large mixed-integer programming model that took as inputs the planned mine layout, projected ore quality, and the project costs for basic mining activities, and produced as an output a near-optimal schedule of activities that maximized discounted ore revenue over a given planning horizon (Carlyle and Eaves, 2001). The insights gained from the use of this model played an important role in determining the company's development strategy.

- *Statistical Software*: When historical data are available, this type of software can often be used to predict future trends. For example, the number of births and deaths in a country could be plotted against time and used to predict the population in a future year. In another example, the U.S. military was faced with a serious shortage of new recruits in 1999. The United States Army Recruiting Command (USAREC) developed tools to track key market intelligence factors. They could not have recruited over 80,000 new soldiers in FY 2000 without the aid of statistical software that identified the trends, wants, and needs of potential recruits (Knowles, et al., 2002).

- *Spreadsheet Software*: This type of software is helpful when the alternatives can easily be arranged in columns, the criteria in rows, and amounts entered in the cells. Spreadsheets are often used to determine what it would take to move a second-place or third-place alternative up to the first place. Spreadsheets can also be used to find out what happens if one factor is weighted differently between the alternatives;

in the tax software, for example, the amount of interest attributed to a spouse could be changed, leading to different amounts of tax owed. In a typical application, Heery International developed and implemented an Excel Spreadsheet optimization model to minimize the total cost of assigning managers to up to 114 construction projects while still maintaining a balanced workload for all their managers. As a result of this model, Heery has been able to manage its projects without having to replace a manager who resigned and has reduced travel costs by assigning managers to projects that are close to their homes (LeBlanc, Randels, and Swann, 2000).

- *Rule-based Software*: This type of software is based on Artificial Intelligence or Expert Systems and is very helpful in dealing with both narrow and broad fields of decision making. An example of a narrow decision focus is whether you will be allowed credit when you swipe your card in a supermarket. An example of a broad field decision focus is deciding whether to launch retaliatory missiles when enemy missiles are detected exploding at military installations.

- *Multi-criteria Decision-Making Software*: This type of software deals with multiple objectives that may have to be attained simultaneously, rather than with a single objective. For example, automobile manufacturers provide railroad companies with annual forecasts of their monthly shipping volumes from various origins to different destinations. The railroad companies jointly operate pools of railcars to transport automobiles. Each pool comprises equipment of a particular type and serves one or more shippers. RELOAD, a fleet management group, manages the repositioning of empty railcars for the carriers. The problem is to find the smallest fleet size that will provide adequate service. The parties involved have agreed on a coordinated use of static and dynamic fleet-sizing models, along with appropriate correction factors, to determine the number of railcars of each type that should be acquired each year. By using this process, the railroad companies have been able to reduce their equipment commitments, saving over a half billion dollars annually (Sherali and Maguire, 2000).

- *Decision-aiding Software*: This type of software focuses on specific subject matter and has been designed to work with only those subjects. Examples include software packages that help decide where to drill an oil well, whether to approve a mortgage loan, or how to prepare the most advantageous tax return. The SLIM (Short cycle time and Low Inventory in Manufacturing) system manages cycle time in semiconductor manufacturing. Between 1996 and 1999, Samsung Electronics Corp. implemented SLIM in all its semiconductor manufacturing facilities, reducing the manufacturing cycle time needed to fabricate dynamic random access memory (DRAM) devices from more than 80 days to under 30 days (Leachman, Kang, and Lin, 2002).

- *Group Decision Support Software*: This type of software helps a group generate alternatives, goals, and constraints, but does not process these to recommend a decision.

- *Enterprise Resource Planning Software*: This complex and sophisticated software has modules that automate and integrate the different functions of a company. It facilitates the flow of information between all areas within a company, such as manufacturing, logistics, finance, and human resources. It is an enterprise-wide information system solution, operating on a common platform, interacting with an integrated set of applications, and consolidating all business operations in a single computing environment. For example, Hyundai has approximately 400 first-tier suppliers, 2,500 second-tier suppliers, and an unknown number of third- or higher-tier suppliers. It has developed mechanisms to coordinate production planning and scheduling activities among its supply-chain members using ERP software (Hahn, Duplaga, and Hartley, 2000). The primary benefit of implementing the software is improved customer satisfaction through better integration of company functions. Another example is Robert Bosch GmbH, which uses the ERP system SAP to cut costs, increase interchangeability of products among the many plants worldwide, and fulfill customer requirements. A manager in the plant describes the advantages of these systems: "Let me tell you what the difference is in our business today versus a year ago, before SAP. I went to our St. Joseph, Michigan, plant and I was talking with the cost accounting person and I asked her about SAP. She has had it now for 9 months and she said, 'I hate it.' And I said, 'Why is that? Is it because we used to have a nice way to put a bill of material in and now you have to go through 4 or 6 screens, so the navigation isn't quite there and SAP is working on it?' She said, 'Oh, no, that doesn't bother me. Earlier, as a cost accounting person, I had my own world there. Everything was wonderful and I booked what I needed to and then at inventory time, we figured out where to match up. I got together with the materials guy once a year and fixed our problems. But now the system is so integrated that I need to stay coordinated every day with the materials guy. I just hate that.'"(Raju and Sankar, 2001).

- *Knowledge Management Software*: This type of software performs as an "intelligent assistant" to provide support for the human expert. It can form a complete, concise, quality-controlled representation of the company's expertise. Each request or input made using these systems would be used to further build and expand the system's database and archive capabilities. The goal of this software is to utilize the company's resources to obtain accurate, detailed, and timely information in order to meet the client's needs.

- *Simulation Software*: Frequently it becomes important to simulate an operation in a computer so that the constraints can be examined more closely. There are many kinds of software available to assist engineers to simulate operating conditions. For example, while it is fun and exciting, engineering in the entertainment industry is also a serious business. Assuring their safety as amusement park visitors roar through roller coaster loops at 60 mph is a demanding responsibility. Fortunately, rapid advances in the field mean that the latest simulation software packages now support sophisticated engineering analyses. However, realizing the full benefits of the latest simulation tools requires extra time and training if engineers are to be able to use them effectively. An engineering simulation using Mechanical Event Simulation (MES) software was developed to verify the integrity of a cinematic motion simulator ride. The results from the model showed that the stresses experienced by the bearings under loading from the six cylinders were within the acceptable range. A comparison of the maximum stresses found in the MES with those of linear static stress analysis showed the static results to be very conservative (Pribonic, 2000).

We will describe two of these methods in detail so that you can use them as you analyze the case studies for this course. However, we would also encourage you to learn more about the other decision support software options and use them during your education and career.

7.5.1 Decision Tree

A Decision Tree is a very helpful software tool that is commonly used by electrical and civil engineers. Decision Trees are excellent tools for helping you choose between several courses of action. They provide a highly effective structure within which you can lay out options and investigate the possible outcomes of each. They also help you form a balanced picture of the risks and rewards associated with each possible course of action.

Drawing a Decision Tree[1]

You start to construct a Decision Tree by defining the decision that you need to make. Draw a small square to represent this on the left edge of a large piece of paper. From this box, draw out lines towards the right for

---

[1] Material in this section is from the website: http://www.mindtools.com/dectree.html

each possible solution and write that solution along the line. Keep the lines as far apart as possible so that you can expand your thoughts. At the end of each line, consider the results. If the result of making that decision is uncertain, draw a small circle. If the result is another decision that you need to make, draw another square. Squares represent decisions, and circles represent uncertain outcomes. Write the decision or the uncertain outcome above the square or circle. If you have completed the solution at the end of the line, just leave it blank.

Starting from the new decision squares on your diagram, draw a fresh set of lines representing the options that you could select. From the circles, draw lines representing possible outcomes. Again make a brief note on each line saying what it means. Keep doing this until you have drawn out as many of the possible outcomes and decisions as you can think of that lead from the original decision.

A Decision Tree describes a list of feasible alternatives, the possible outcomes associated with each alternative, the corresponding probabilities, and costs. As an example, we will evaluate two alternative designs for constructing a building using a Decision Tree. Design I is based on conventional procedure, has a probability of satisfactory performance of 99%, and costs $1.5 million. Design II is a more modern design and is expected to reduce the cost of construction to $1 million. However, the reliability of Design II is not known. If the assumptions made by an engineer for Design II are valid, the reliability of the building performing satisfactorily is 99%. If that engineer's assumptions are invalid, the reliability of the building performing satisfactorily is 90%. The engineer is only 50% sure of these assumptions. If the building does not perform satisfactorily, in either Design I or Design II, your company is obligated to spend an additional $10 million to destroy and recreate the building (Ang and Tang, 1975). Your task is to choose one of the designs. A Decision Tree for this problem is shown in Figure 22.

Figure 22: Decision Tree for Design Problem

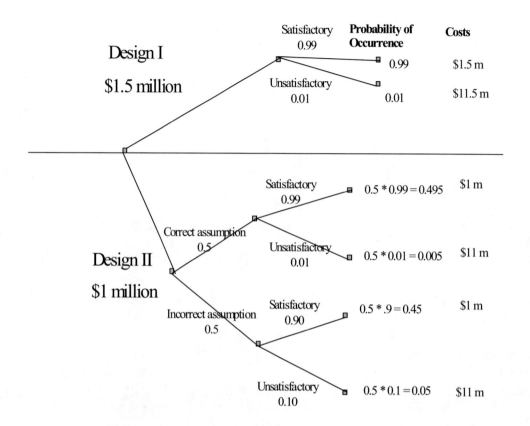

The probabilities for the end leaves are computed by multiplying the probability of the leaves on the branch. For example, the probability of Design II being satisfactory (prob=0.99) given that your assumptions are correct (prob=0.5) is 0.99*0.5 = 0.495.

Based on the Decision Tree, we can compute the expected cost of the building. For the first design, the cost of the building is $1.5 million if the design is satisfactory and $11.5 million if the design is unsatisfactory, since the building would be constructed for $1.5 million and then reconstructed, costing an extra $10 million. Expected costs for choosing Design I are computed by multiplying the probability by the cost of each alternative:

- Expected cost for choosing Design I:
  = 0.99 * $1.5 Million + 0.01 * $11.5 Million = $1.6 Million

Similarly, the expected cost of choosing Design II is computed by multiplying the probabilities with the cost of alternatives. The cost of construction, if satisfactory is $1 million and, if unsatisfactory, is $11

165

million ($1 million for the original construction plus $10 million for reconstruction). The expected costs for choosing Design II are computed by multiplying the probability by the cost of each alternative.

- Expected cost for choosing Design II:
  = 0.495 * $1 Million + 0.005 * $11 Million
  + 0.45 * $1 Million + 0.05 * $11 Million = $1.55 Million

Based on the computations, the expected cost of choosing Design II is lower by $.05 million than Design I. As an engineer, this Decision Tree has provided you with a justification for the choice of Design II. However, you have to temper this judgement with other factors such as the risk-taking ability of your organization, financial constraints, and the effects on the environment; you can easily change the results of the analysis to favor Design I if you change the values of some of the probabilities.

Figure 23: Decision Tree for Modified Design

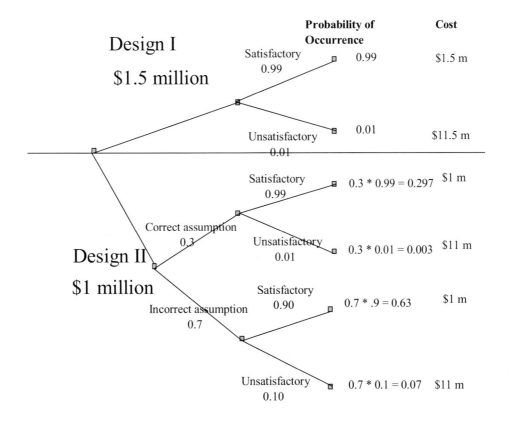

For example, if the engineer changes the probability that his/her assumption might be valid to 0.3 instead of 0.5, the Decision Tree changes

166

as shown in Figure 23. The computation of the expected cost for Design II will also change.

- Expected cost for choosing Design II:
  = 0.297 * $1 Million + 0.003 * $11 Million
  + 0.63 * $1 Million + 0.07 * $11 Million = $1.73 Million

In this case, Design I becomes the more favorable solution since its expected cost is $1.6 million, $0.13 million less than for Design II. Similarly, changing the other probability values will change your ultimate decision.

These two Decision Tree examples illustrate how it is possible to favor different alternatives depending on the probabilities that are assigned to the events. There are additional practice examples at the end of this chapter where you can practice your skills in constructing Decision Trees. The Decision Tree software is available for purchase or as freeware from many different companies, some of whom are listed at the end of this chapter.

7.5.2: Multi-Criteria Decision Making Software

Most decisions are much more complex than the one discussed in the previous section. To deal with such situations, Multi-Criteria Decision-Making software is used. The software in this category assists a decision-maker in solving complex problems involving many criteria and several possible courses of action. It provides the tools to construct decision frameworks for both routine and non-routine problems and to utilize these decision frameworks in ways that incorporate your own value judgements. An example of a multi-criteria decision-making software package is *Expert Choice*, which is based on the theory of Analytic Hierarchy Process, AHP (Saaty, 1980; Saaty, 1982).

AHP theory is based on the three principles of constructing hierarchies, establishing priorities, and logical consistency. The first principle expects you to deconstruct complex reality into its constituent parts, and these in turn into their parts, and so on hierarchically. By breaking down reality into homogeneous clusters and subdividing these clusters into smaller ones, large amounts of information can be integrated into the structure of a problem. In the software, this framework is shown as a hierarchy that is used to organize all the relevant factors to solve a problem in a logical and systematic way, from the goal, to the criteria, to the subcriteria, and so on, down to the alternatives of a decision. First you must define the problem, then you enter all the relevant issues into the hierarchy.

We will use the Expert Choice software to illustrate a multi-criteria decision. When you buy a car, you usually have several criteria or objectives to satisfy before you are willing to buy the car. For this example, we will use the objectives of *price, quality*, and *prestige* as the most important criteria for purchasing a car. If you were to choose other criteria, the results from the model would be different.

The first level of the hierarchy contains the goal of the decision: choose the best car for a student to buy. The next level of hierarchy has the three criteria: price, quality, and prestige. We can further refine the criteria of quality into the sub-criteria of design, comfort, and safety. Say, for example, that you are using this decision model to choose among four different cars: Cavalier, Accord, Neon, and Volvo S40. The alternatives are shown at the bottom of the hierarchy. Figure 24 shows how the "Expert Choice" model depicts this problem and structures the model.

The second principle of the "Expert Choice" software perceives relationships among the options, comparing pairs of similar options against certain criteria and discriminating between both members of a pair by judging the intensity of preference for one over the other. The user provides judgements on the elements of the hierarchy in pairs according to their relative importance. For the car-buying example, this implies comparing the priorities among the nodes (price, quality, and prestige) in the hierarchy chart shown in Figure 24.

Figure 24: AHP Model for Buying a Car

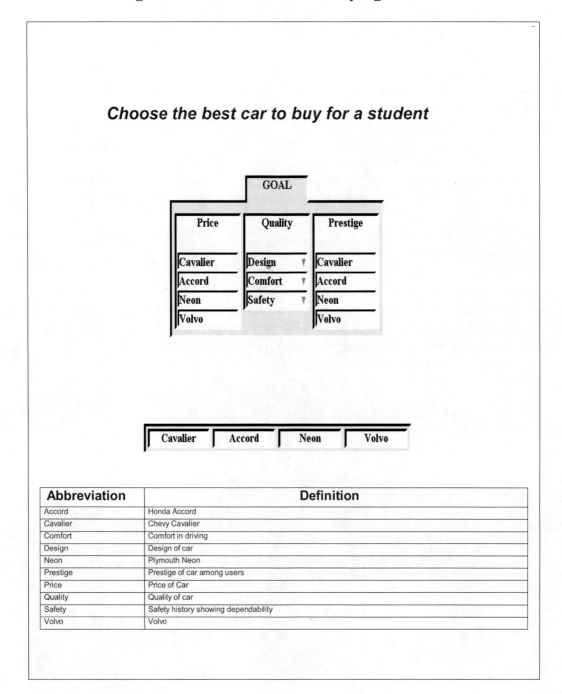

Choose the best car to buy for a student

Abbreviation	Definition
Accord	Honda Accord
Cavalier	Chevy Cavalier
Comfort	Comfort in driving
Design	Design of car
Neon	Plymouth Neon
Prestige	Prestige of car among users
Price	Price of Car
Quality	Quality of car
Safety	Safety history showing dependability
Volvo	Volvo

Figure 25: Comparing Price of the Cars

Choose the best car to buy for a student

Node: 10000

Data with respect to: Price < GOAL

Cavalier	10000.
Accord	14000.
Neon	11200.
Volvo	24000.

Abbreviation	Definition
Goal	Choose the best car to buy for a student
Price	Price of Car
Cavalier	Chevy Cavalier
Accord	Honda Accord
Neon	Plymouth Neon
Volvo	Volvo

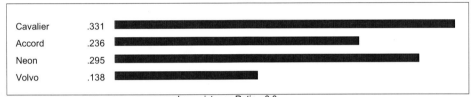

Cavalier	.331
Accord	.236
Neon	.295
Volvo	.138

Inconsistency Ratio =0.0

170

Figure 26: Comparing Design Features of the Cars

Choose the best car to buy for a student

Node: 21000

Compare the relative PREFERENCE with respect to   : Design < Quality < GOAL

	Accord	Neon	Volvo
Cavalier	(2.0)	1.0	(4.0)
Accord		2.0	(3.0)
Neon			(3.0)

Row element is __ times more than column element unless enclosed in ()

Abbreviation	Definition
Goal	Choose the best car to buy for a student
Quality	Quality of car
Design	Design of car
Cavalier	Chevy Cavalier
Accord	Honda Accord
Neon	Plymouth Neon
Volvo	Volvo

Cavalier	.124
Accord	.226
Neon	.134
Volvo	.517

Inconsistency Ratio =0.02

The price of all four cars is known and is used to make a priority assessment in Figure 25. Since the price of the Cavalier is the lowest ($10,000), its priority is highest (0.331), while the price of the Volvo S40 ($24,000) is the highest, leading to a low price priority (0.138). Similarly, the priorities among the four cars based on their design are shown in Figure 26. This shows that the Volvo S40 is preferred three times more than the Neon based on the design features, the Accord is preferred two times more than the Neon, and so on. In a similar manner, the priority for each of the nodes is worked out with respect to the nodes below it.

The third principle of the Expert Choice model is to establish relationships among objects in such a way that they are coherent and consistent. The process reveals any inconsistencies and requests the user to make the appropriate changes. The software determines if these comparisons are logical and consistent and computes an "inconsistency index." This measure is helpful in identifying possible errors in judgement as well as inconsistencies in the judgements themselves. A selection with an "inconsistency index" less than 0.1, is considered acceptable. If the inconsistency index is more than 0.1, then a re-examination of the judgements is in order.

Figure 27: High Inconsistency Ratio for Comfort

Choose the best car to buy for a student

Compare the relative PREFERENCE with respect to: Comfort < Quality < GOAL

	Accord	Neon	Volvo
Cavalier	2.0	(3.0)	(2.0)
Accord		1.0	2.0
Neon			2.0

Row element is __ times more than column element unless enclosed in ()

Abbreviation	Definition
Goal	Choose the best car to buy for a student
Quality	Quality of car
Comfort	Comfort in driving
Cavalier	Chevy Cavalier
Accord	Honda Accord
Neon	Plymouth Neon
Volvo	Volvo

Cavalier	.201
Accord	.244
Neon	.355
Volvo	.200

Inconsistency Ratio =0.19

Figure 27 shows an example of a high inconsistency ratio. There may be errors in the judgments themselves, inconsistencies between the judgments, or both; the number computed by the software is simply an overall consistency index. The decision-maker has to revisit the prioritization process and check the preferences, reassessing and correcting any errors that may have occurred during the judging process.

In this example, the inconsistency ratio for the comfort criteria is shown as 0.19. Examining the preferences chosen, the Cavalier was preferred twice as much as the Accord in terms of its comfort and the Accord is preferred twice as much as the Volvo S40. Thus, the software expects that the Cavalier will be deemed to be more comfortable than the Volvo S40. However, we judged the Volvo S40 to be twice as

Figure 28: Correct Rating of Cars Based on Comfort

Choose the best car to buy for a student

Node: 22000

Compare the relative PREFERENCE with respect to: Comfort < Quality < GOAL

	Accord	Neon	Volvo
Cavalier	(2.0)	(3.0)	(2.0)
Accord		1.0	2.0
Neon			2.0

Row element is __ times more than column element unless enclosed in ()

Abbreviation	Definition
Goal	Choose the best car to buy for a student
Quality	Quality of car
Comfort	Comfort in driving
Cavalier	Chevy Cavalier
Accord	Honda Accord
Neon	Plymouth Neon
Volvo	Volvo

Cavalier	.124	
Accord	.326	
Neon	.356	
Volvo	.194	

Inconsistency Ratio =0.02

comfortable as the Cavalier. The high inconsistency ratio points out this error in judgment. When we examine the table, we find that we intended to say that the Accord was twice as comfortable as the Cavalier, but made a mistake in our data entry. Once this is corrected, the inconsistency ratio drops to 0.02, as shown in Figure 8. Figure 2 rates the four cars based on safety factors.

Figure 29: Rating of Cars based on Safety

Choose the best car to buy for a student

Node: 23000

Compare the relative PREFERENCE with respect to: Safety < Quality < GOAL

	Accord	Neon	Volvo
Cavalier	(4.0)	(3.0)	(7.0)
Accord		2.0	1.0
Neon			(2.0)

Row element is __ times more than column element unless enclosed in ()

Abbreviation	Definition
Goal	Choose the best car to buy for a student
Quality	Quality of car
Safety	Safety history showing dependability
Cavalier	Chevy Cavalier
Accord	Honda Accord
Neon	Plymouth Neon
Volvo	Volvo

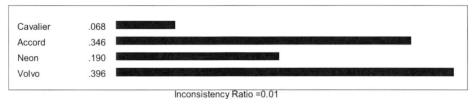

Cavalier	.068
Accord	.346
Neon	.190
Volvo	.396

Inconsistency Ratio =0.01

Figure 30: Rating of Cars Based on Prestige

Choose the best car to buy for a student

Node: 30000

Compare the relative PREFERENCE with respect to: Prestige < GOAL

	Accord	Neon	Volvo
Cavalier	(2.0)	(3.0)	(9.0)
Accord		(2.0)	(6.0)
Neon			(6.0)

Row element is __ times more than column element unless enclosed in ()

Abbreviation	Definition
Goal	Choose the best car to buy for a student
Prestige	Prestige of car among users
Cavalier	Chevy Cavalier
Accord	Honda Accord
Neon	Plymouth Neon
Volvo	Volvo

Cavalier	.058
Accord	.101
Neon	.160
Volvo	.681

Inconsistency Ratio =0.03

Figure 30 rates the four cars based on their prestige and Figure 31 compares the importance of the three major categories of price, quality, and prestige for the prospective car buyer.

Figure 31: Rating of Cars Based on Major Factors

Choose the best car to buy for a student

Compare the relative IMPORTANCE with respect to: GOAL

Node: 0

	Quality	Prestige
Price	1.0	9.0
Quality		5.0

Row element is __ times more than column element unless enclosed in ()

Abbreviation	Definition
Goal	Choose the best car to buy for a student
Price	Price of Car
Quality	Quality of car
Prestige	Prestige of car among users

Price	.511
Quality	.420
Prestige	.069

Inconsistency Ratio =0.04

Finally, all the pairwise comparisons are synthesized to rank the alternatives overall based on the theoretical principles of the Analytic Hierarchy Process (Saaty, 1980). The result is a set of priorities for the alternatives that are ratio scale numbers. If alternative A has a final priority of 0.40 and alternative B has a priority of 0.20, then A is not only better in some vague sense, but also is twice as good as B. Such ratio scale measurements are both powerful and capable of unifying measurements. Figures 32 and 33 show the synthesis of all the options for the car-buying example.

Figure 32: Synthesis of Judgements –Sideways View

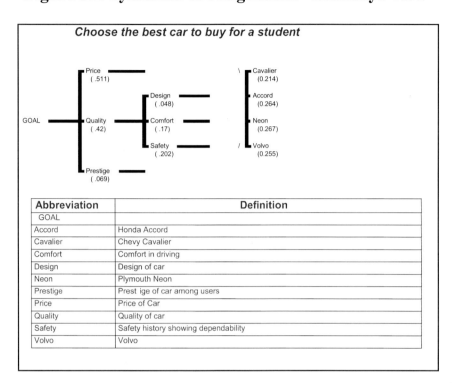

Choose the best car to buy for a student

Abbreviation	Definition
GOAL	
Accord	Honda Accord
Cavalier	Chevy Cavalier
Comfort	Comfort in driving
Design	Design of car
Neon	Plymouth Neon
Prestige	Prest ige of car among users
Price	Price of Car
Quality	Quality of car
Safety	Safety history showing dependability
Volvo	Volvo

Figures 32 and 33 show that given the judgments entered in the model, the Neon is the best buy for this student with a priority of 0.267. The figures show that the Neon has a high priority of 0.267 followed by 0.264 for the Accord, 0.255 for the Volvo S40 and 0.214 for the Cavalier.

The software also provides sensitivity analysis capabilities so that you can change the weights of the criteria and see the impact on the final choice. Expert Choice does not make a choice for you, but helps you to make an informed choice based on your knowledge, experiences, and preferences. Figure 34 repeats the solution given earlier in Figures 32 and 3 3 and shows that the student should prefer the Neon given that price, quality, and prestige were rated at 51.1%, 42%, and 6.9% importance, respectively.

Figure 33: Synthesis of Judgements - Tree-Leaf View

Choose the best car to buy for a student

Synthesis of Leaf Nodes with respect to GOAL
Distributive Mode
OVERALL INCONSISTENCY INDEX = 0.02

LEVEL 1	LEVEL 2	LEVEL 3	LEVEL 4	LEVEL 5
Price =.511				
	Cavalier=.169			
	Neon =.151			
	Accord =.121			
	Volvo =.070			
Quality =.420				
	Safety =.202			
		Volvo =.080		
		Accord =.070		
		Neon =.038		
		Cavalier=.014		
	Comfort =.170			
		Neon =.061		
		Accord =.055		
		Volvo =.033		
		Cavalier=.021		
	Design =.048			
		Volvo =.025		
		Accord =.011		
		Neon =.006		
		Cavalier=.006		
Prestige=.069				
	Volvo =.047			
	Neon =.011			
	Accord =.007			
	Cavalier=.004			

Neon	.267	
Accord	.264	
Volvo	.255	
Cavalier	.214	

At what ratio of the factors does the Volvo S40 become the best choice? Figure 35 shows that if the ratio of price, quality, and prestige weights were changed to 50.5%, 40%, and 9.6%, then the Volvo S40 is the best choice, at a 26 % rating.

Figure 34: High Priority for Price & Quality Leads to Neon as the Choice

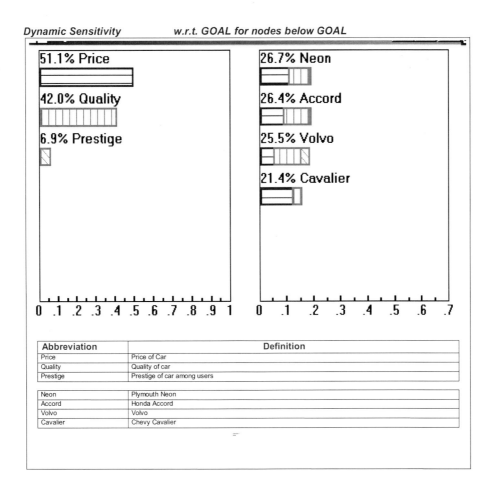

Figure 36 shows that when the quality rating is increased to 45%, the Accord becomes the best choice, at a rating of 26.7%, and Figure 37 shows that when the weight for price is increased to 81.1%, the Cavalier becomes the best choice, at a rating of 28.6%. These figures explain why we sometimes make choices that are not intuitively clear to others; the model makes it possible to make the choice process explicit and enables us to explain our choice process better.

Figure 35: Higher Priority for Prestige Leads to Volvo as the Choice

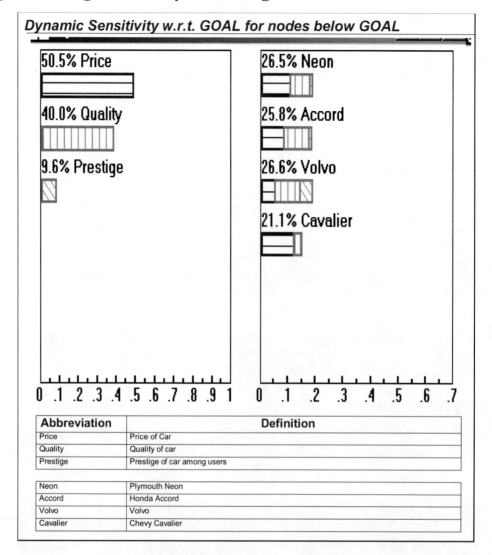

Figure 36: Higher Priority for Quality Leads to Accord as the Choice

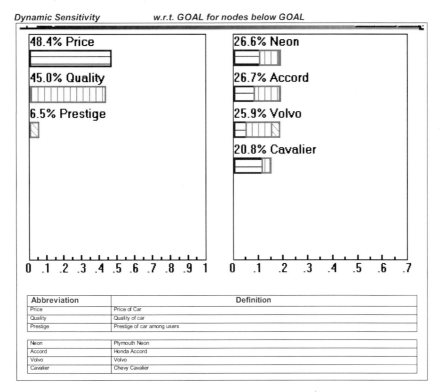

Abbreviation	Definition
Price	Price of Car
Quality	Quality of car
Prestige	Prestige of car among users

Neon	Plymouth Neon
Accord	Honda Accord
Volvo	Volvo
Cavalier	Chevy Cavalier

Figure 37: Higher Priority for Price Leads to Cavalier as the Choice

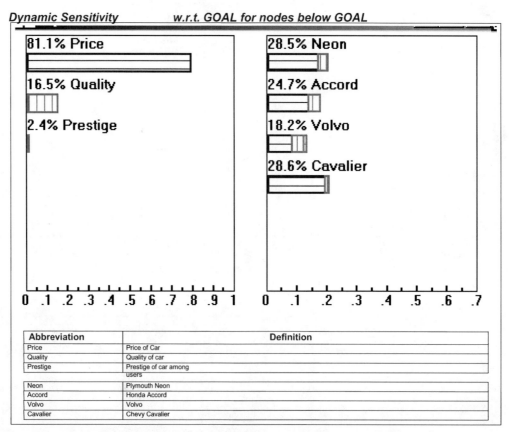

Abbreviation	Definition
Price	Price of Car
Quality	Quality of car
Prestige	Prestige of car among users
Neon	Plymouth Neon
Accord	Honda Accord
Volvo	Volvo
Cavalier	Chevy Cavalier

The Expert Choice software has been applied in hundreds of business and government decision applications, including total quality management, resource allocation, cost benefit analysis, "what-if" forecasting, and product research and development.

7.6 OTHER CONSIDERATIONS IN DECISION-MAKING PROCESSES

In the great majority of cases, individuals do not use the decision support software discussed in the earlier sections to make decisions. Frequently, we make decisions based on other factors such as "intuition," "gut feeling," "follow the leader," "follow the dominant personality," etc. When you observe such a situation, it is important to realize that there are a few well-established biases that run counter to our "intuition" or "common sense." This section discusses a few of them.

Tversky and Kahneman (1986) have shown that there are three major differences between using decision-support software and the process by which individuals make decisions:

181

(a) People think of consequences as increments (or decrements) to current wealth and have an aversion to losses; therefore, people tend to favor incremental decisions over radically new decisions.

(b) People tend not to distinguish adequately the dimensionality between large numbers; i.e., they may have the impression that a thrust of three million pounds is a lot like a thrust of three hundred thousand pounds.

(c) People frequently give unlikely events more weight than they deserve, and give correspondingly less weight to very likely events. That is, they may consider the probability of being involved in a plane disaster to be much higher than that of being involved in an automobile accident.

Also people's assumptions and their ability to evaluate probabilities are often questionable. Bell et al., (1988) found that:

(a) People have poor intuitions about probability. For example, a gambler may say, "I've had a couple of successes and, therefore, I am due for a failure." Alternatively, he or she may believe the counter fallacy, "The dice are running hot. Let me play again."

(b) Lay people and experts alike do not calibrate well. By and large the probability distributions they assign are too narrow and tight; people thus think that they know more than they really know and are surprised far too often.

(c) It is very hard to assess small probabilities, such as 1 in a million.

(d) Feelings of anxiety, joy, anticipation, regret, disappointment, elation, and envy are a constant part of human life but are not accounted for by the decision models.

(e) People may arrive at opposite conclusions when data are presented in different ways.

(f) Cultural background has a strong influence on the decision-making processes of individuals.

(g) Men and women use different criteria in making decisions and exhibit different behavioral patterns in group decision-making contexts.

(h) Social upbringing restricts people from accepting nontraditional solutions to problems.

182

We hope that you will include these considerations when faced with decision-making situations and make good decisions based on a proper balance between the scientific and intuitive decision-making processes.

7.7 SUMMARY

In this chapter, we described the steps in the prescriptive decision-making process: understand the situation, identify the problem, identify alternatives, evaluate each alternative, choose the best alternative, implement a decision, monitor performance, and obtain feedback. We also discussed the different kinds of methods that are available to help you solve real-world engineering problems. These methods include: Decision Trees, linear programming, statistical software, spreadsheet-based software, rule-based software, multi-criteria decision-making software, group decision support systems, enterprise resource planning software, knowledge management software, and simulation software.

We also explained how to construct and use a Decision Tree and provided examples to illustrate this method. The use of the Expert Choice software package, a decision support system, was explored using an example that showed the decision process involved in buying a car. Finally, the intuitive considerations that also need to be included in decision-making were explained.

As an engineer you may have to wrestle with technical, managerial, ethical, financial, interpersonal, political, and scheduling factors when making decisions that will affect the success of your career, company, and product. The software discussed in this chapter could provide you with valuable assistance as you make these decisions.

SHORT ESSAY QUESTIONS

1) What is the name of the field that studies decision-making?

2) What are the steps in decision-making?

3) Describe each step in decision-making process.

4) Take a problem you have solved in the past (such as choosing a college, getting a job, etc.,) and use the steps of the decision-making process to analyze it. Did the analysis help you improve your decision-making process?

5) Find examples of good and poor decision-making from newspaper articles or practitioner journals. Analyze them and identify the lessons

that could be learned by the organization concerned.

6) Analyze each company example (Boxes 2-1 through 2-4) with respect to the steps involved in the decision-making process and describe how you would make the choice given the same problem.

7) Define a Decision Tree.

8) Define probability and give an example of how to use this concept.

9) Your design of equipment to clear the trees on campus of toilet paper after victorious football games costs $200,000. There is a probability of 0.05 that it may not work. The cost for facilities personnel to clean up after each game without your machine is $50,000 and the team wins an average of eight games per season. The cost for personnel to clean up with your machine is only $5,000. Should the university invest in building your machine?

10) A waste treatment process is being created for Gadsen, AL. Given that it is a new plant, its utilization is unknown. You have a choice of designing a small unit X or a larger unit Y. You have estimated the utilization of this unit for two levels, high and low. You estimate that there is a probability of 60% that the utilization of the proposed treatment process will be high. The cost of unit X is $0.5 million, but it is designed for low utilization. If you want to change the unit to high utilization, it will cost an additional $1.5 million. Unit Y costs $1 million and it is designed for high utilization; it will cost an additional 0.25 million if it has to be used in a low utilization mode. Which unit will you select based on the expected cost for the plant? What happens if the estimate of the probability changes to a 40% chance that the process will be highly utilized? What happens if the estimate of the probability becomes 80% that the process will be highly utilized?

11) Hurricanes have long been a threat to the east coast of the USA. The average annual property damage is estimated to be $900 million. A private company has come up with a seeding technology so that the forces of the hurricane could be dispersed before it hits the coast. Observations have shown that wind speeds usually decrease with seeding of the clouds; but there is a possibility that the wind speed may actually increase after seeding. If the seeding leads to lower wind speed, a saving of 20% in damage costs is expected. If the seeding leads to a higher wind speed, a further loss of 40% is expected. The cost to seed is $100 million per year, and the insurance companies have agreed to give the excess savings or pass on the excess loss to the seeding company every year. Given the following probabilities, is it profitable for the company to seed?
   A) Probability of 0.1 that high winds will result.

B) Probability of 0.5 that high winds will result.

C) Probability of 0.01 that high winds will result.

D) Suppose a new seeding technology has been created (at a cost of $200 million per year) that will reduce the wind speed, resulting in saving of 80%. Would you fund this experimental technology given the above probabilities?

12) Define a decision support system.

13) Discuss the various kinds of decision support systems software that are available to assist engineers in their jobs.

14) Discuss the alternative hierarchy process.

15) Could the Expert Choice Software replace a human decision-maker? If so, under what conditions?

16) What are the steps that must be followed when using the Expert Choice software?

17) What are the psychological aspects that need to be considered in decision-making scenarios?

18) What do you think engineers do in their jobs?

19) Do engineers make decisions? If so, what kind of decisions?

REFERENCES

Ang, A.H., and Tang, W.H., Probability Concepts in Engineering Planning and Design, Wiley, New York, NY, 1975.

Badawy, M.K. *Developing Managerial Skills in Engineers and Scientists*, Van Nostrand Reinhold, New York, NY, 1995.

Bell, D.E., Raiffa, H. and Tversky, A. *Decision Making: Descriptive, Normative, and Prescriptive Interactions*, Cambridge University Press, Cambridge, UK, 1988.

Carlyle, W.M. and Eaves, B.C. Underground Planning at Stillwater Mining Company, *Interfaces*, 31(4): July-Aug. 2001, pp. 50-60.

Clemen, R.T. *Making Hard Decisions*, Wadsworth Publishing Co., Belmont, CA, 1996.

Dey, P.K., Quantitative Risk Management Aids Refinery Construction, *Hydrocarbon Processing*, March 2002, pp. 85-95.

Hahn, C.K., Duplaga, E.A., and Hartley, J.L. Supply-Chain Synchronization: Lessons from Hyundai Motor Company, *Interfaces*, 30(4): July-Aug. 2000, pp. 32-45.

Leachman, R.C., Kang, J., and Lin, V., SLIM: Short Cycle Time and Low Inventory in Manufacturing at Samsung Electronics, *Interfaces*, 32(1): Jan-Feb. 2002, pp. 61-77.

LeBlanc, L.J., Randels, D. and Swann, T.K. Heery International's Spreadsheet Optimization Model for Assigning Managers to Construction Projects, *Interfaces*, 30(6): Nov.-Dec. 2000, pp. 95-106.

Kleindorfer, P.R., Kunreuther, H.C., and Schoemaker, P.J. H, *Decision Sciences: An Integrative Perspective*, Cambridge University Press, New York, NY 1993.

Knowles, J.A., Parlier, G.H., Hoscheit, G.C., Ayer, R., Lyman, K., and Fancher, R., Reinventing Army Recruiting, *Interfaces*, 32(1): Jan-Feb. 2002, pp. 78-92.

Pribonic, E. Rock and Roll Engineering, *Design Engineering*, June 2000, p. 33.

Rau, K-H, R. and Sankar, C.S. Multiple Information Systems Coping with a Growing and Changing Business: Robert Bosch Corporation, *Journal of SMET Education: Innovations and Research,* 2(3&4): Sept-Dec 2001, pp. 19-36.

Saaty, T.L. *Decision Making for Leaders*, Lifetime Learning Publications, Belmont, CA., 1982.

Saaty, T.L. *The Analytic Hierarchy Process*, McGraw-Hill, New York, NY, 1980.

Sherali, H.D. and Maguire, L.W. Determining Rail Size Fleet Sizes for Shipping Automobiles, *Interfaces*, 30(6): Nov-Dec 2000, pp. 80-90.

Simon, H.A. *Models of Man*, Wiley Publishers, New York, NY, 1957.

Sorensen, T.C. *Decision-Making in the White House: The Olive Branch or the Arrows*, Columbia University Press, New York, 1963.

Tversky, A and Kahneman, D. Rational Choice and the Framing of Decisions, *Journal of Business*, 59(4), Part 2, 5251-78, 1986.

Twiss, B.C. *Business for Engineers*, Peter Peregrinus Ltd., London, UK, 1988.

COMPANIES THAT SELL DECISION TREE SOFTWARE

www.smartdraw.com: With this software you can draw flowcharts, Organization Charts, Networks, Forms, Floor Plans, Time Lines, Presentations, and Decision Trees.

www.palisade.com: PrecisionTree® is the Decision Analysis Add-In for Microsoft Excel®. It enables you to build Decision Trees and influence diagrams directly in your spreadsheet. Diagrams can be created by selecting cells in your spreadsheet and clicking node buttons at the PrecisionTree toolbar. Probabilities and payoffs are entered directly in the cells in your tree. With one click, PrecisionTree will run a powerful decision analysis on your model, determining the best way to proceed with your decision.

http://www.cs.umass.edu/~lrn/iti/L ITI (Incremental Tree Inducer) is a program that constructs Decision Trees automatically from labeled examples. Although the program is called ITI, it includes both the ITI and DMTI (Direct Metric Tree Induction) algorithms. You can run the ITI program, and then use command options to invoke the DMTI algorithm within.

http://www.treeage.com/: DATA Interactive™ – allows you to create your own decision analysis applications for the Internet, intranet, or CD-ROM, using Decision Trees built in DATA.

http://faculty.fuqua.duke.edu/daweb/dasw6.htm: Provides a list of Decision Tree software that is available for purchase.

COMPANIES THAT SELL DECISION SUPPORT SYSTEMS

http://www.expertchoice.com: Expert Choice is a group meta decision support software product based on the world's most successful decision-making methodology, the Analytic Hierarchy Process (AHP). Expert Choice enables you to leverage the expertise and collective wisdom of your team for more informed and justifiable decisions.

http://www.outlooksoft.com: EAP is a unified, real-time business performance management solution that delivers decision support features and functionality.

http://www.knowledgestorm.com: Provides a link to many different decision support systems that are available in the market.

APPENDIX 1: EXAMPLES OF THE USE OF SCIENTIFIC DECISION MAKING IN ENGINEERING

INTERFACES 31:1 Jan 2001 pp:91-107

Rightsizing and management of prototype vehicle testing at Ford Motor Company

Kenneth Chelst, John Sidelko, Alex Przebienda, Jeffrey Lockledge, and Dimitrios Mihailidis

The prototype vehicles that Ford Motor Company uses to verify new designs are a major annual investment. A team of engineering managers studying for master's degrees in a Wayne State University program taught at Ford adapted a classroom set-covering example to begin development of the prototype optimization model (POM). Ford uses the POM and its related expert systems to budget, plan, and manage prototype test fleets and to maintain testing integrity, reducing annual prototype costs by more than $250 million. POM's first use on the European Transit vehicle reduced costs by an estimated $12 million. The model dramatically shortened the planning process, established global procedures, and created a common structure for dialogue between budgeting and engineering.

INTERFACES 27:1 Jan 1997 pp:71-88

Pontis: a system for maintenance optimization and improvement of US bridge networks

Kamal Golabi and Richard Shepard

Pontis provides a systematic methodology for allocating funds, evaluating current and future needs of bridges and options to meet those needs, and recommending the optimal policy for each bridge in the context of overall network benefits, budgets, and restrictions. After a trial implementation in California and extensive testing in several states, the system was adopted by AASHTO (Association of American State Highway Officials). Currently, over 40 states are implementing Pontis. At the heart of Pontis is a set of predictive and optimization models which derive their information from judgmental, engineering, and economic models and various databases. The predictive models start with engineering-based subjective inputs and update themselves in a Bayesian context as data is collected. The optimization models consist of interrelated Markov decision models and mathematical programming tools and models.

APPENDIX 2: EXAMPLE OF HOW FACTORS OTHER THAN ENGINEERING INFLUENCE THE SUCCESS/FAILURE OF A COMPANY

The Demise of Shiva Corporation: High-Tech Solutions that Did not Succeed in the Marketplace

Shiva Corporation was a leading global provider of remote access solutions for business. The company was founded in 1985 and was based in Bedford, MA. The company derived its revenues from remote access products and other communications products and services. The company's products were used to create a new Virtual Private Network (VPN) that can be used to connect people over long distances via the Internet. They expected to provide a single solution that would enable their customers to manage both direct dial and VPN connections from the same terminal, using the same authentication list and security software. Their technology would allow "long distance" remote access connections to be placed for the cost of a local call. They expected this integration of direct dial and VPN would help customers lower the overall cost of managing their solutions. *PC Magazine* chose the Shiva LANRover Access Switch as the top performer on their tests during 1997. The system offered client-side caching to speed throughput, tariff management to control costs, dial-in, dial-out, and LAN-to-LAN routing for flexibility.

Financial information from the company for five years is shown below (in $million):

	Jan-Oct 1998	1997	1996	1995	1994	1993
Total Revenues	$108	$144	$200	$118	$81	$61
Operating income (loss)	(22)	(26)	(23)	(4)	(4)	2
Income (loss) before income taxes	(18)	(22)	26	(3)	3	0.7
Income tax provision (benefit)	(6)	(8)	9	2	1	0.3
Net income (loss)	(12)	(14)	17	(1)	2	0.4
Net income (loss) per share - Basic	(0.4)	(0.47)	0.59	(0.19)	0.16	0.04
Market price of share: **High:** **Low:**	14.38 2.75	36.75 8.06	87.25 25.13			